MW01251176

Loyola University Chicago
Chicago, Illinois

Written by Nathan Ramin
Edited by Kevan Gray

Additional contributions by Adam Burns, Omid Gohari,
Christina Koshzow, Chris Mason, Joey Rahimi, Jon Skindzier,
Luke Skurman, Tim Williams, Asad Samar,
Kimberly Moore and Kristen Burns

ISBN # 1-59658-077-1
ISSN # 1551-1095
© Copyright 2005 College Prowler
All Rights Reserved
Printed in the U.S.A.
www.collegeprowler.com

Special thanks to Babs Carryer, Andy Hannah, LaunchCyte, Tim O'Brien, Bob Sehlinger, Thomas Emerson, Andrew Skurman, Barbara Skurman, Bert Mann, Dave Lehman, Daniel Fayock, Chris Babyak, The Donald H. Jones Center for Entrepreneurship, Terry Slease, Jerry McGinnis, Bill Ecenberger, Idie McGinty, Kyle Russell, Jacque Zaremba, Larry Winderbaum, Paul Kelly, Roland Allen, Jon Reider, Team Evankovich, Julie Fenstermaker, Lauren Varacalli, Abu Noaman, Jason Putorti, Mark Exler, Daniel Steinmeyer, Jared Cohon, Gabriela Oates, Tri Ad Litho, David Koegler, and Glen Meakem.

Bounce Back Team: Katie Greaney, Ryan Fischer, Nick Zeigler

College Prowler™
5001 Baum Blvd.
Suite 456
Pittsburgh, PA 15213

Phone: (412) 697-1390, 1(800) 290-2682
Fax: (412) 697-1396, 1(800) 772-4972
E-mail: info@collegeprowler.com
Website: www.collegeprowler.com

College Prowler™ is not sponsored by, affiliated with, or approved by Loyola University of Chicago in any way.

College Prowler™ strives faithfully to record its sources. As the reader understands, opinions, impressions, and experiences are necessarily personal and unique. Accordingly, there are, and can be, no guarantees of future satisfaction extended to the reader.

© Copyright 2005 College Prowler. All rights reserved. No part of this work may be reproduced or transmitted in any form or by any means, including but not limited to, photocopy, recording, or any information storage and retrieval systems, without the express written permission of College Prowler™.

Welcome to College Prowler™

During the writing of College Prowler's guidebooks, we felt it was critical that our content was unbiased and unaffiliated with any college or university. We think it's important that our readers get honest information and a realistic impression of the student opinions on any campus — that's why if any aspect of a particular school is terrible, we (unlike a campus brochure) intend to publish it. While we do keep an eye out for the occasional extremist — the cheerleader or the cynic — we take pride in letting the students tell it like it is. We strive to create a book that's as representative as possible of each particular campus. Our books cover both the good and the bad, and whether the survey responses point to recurring trends or a variation in opinion, these sentiments are directly and proportionally expressed through our guides.

College Prowler guidebooks are in the hands of students throughout the entire process of their creation. Because you can't make student-written guides without the students, we have students at each campus who help write, randomly survey their peers, edit, layout, and perform accuracy checks on every book that we publish. From the very beginning, student writers gather the most up-to-date stats, facts, and inside information on their colleges. They fill each section with student quotes and summarize the findings in editorial reviews. In addition, each school receives a collection of letter grades (A through F) that reflect student opinion and help to represent contentment, prominence, or satisfaction for each of our 20 specific categories. Just as in grade school, the higher the mark the more content, more prominent, or more satisfied the students are with the particular category.

Once a book is written, additional students serve as editors and check for accuracy even more extensively. Our bounce-back team — a group of randomly selected students who have no involvement with the project — are asked to read over the material in order to help ensure that the book accurately expresses every aspect of the university and its students. This same process is applied to the 200-plus schools College Prowler currently covers. Each book is the result of endless student contributions, hundreds of pages of research and writing, and countless hours of hard work. All of this has led to the creation of a student information network that stretches across the nation to every school that we cover. It's no easy accomplishment, but it's the reason that our guides are such a great resource.

When reading our books and looking at our grades, keep in mind that every college is different and that the students who make up each school are not uniform — as a result, it is important to assess schools on a case-by-case basis. Because it's impossible to summarize an entire school with a single number or description, each book provides a dialogue, not a decision, that's made up of 20 different topics and hundreds of student quotes. In the end, we hope that this guide will serve as a valuable tool in your college selection process. Enjoy!

OMID GOHARI ◯ CHRISTINA KOSHZOW ◯ CHRIS MASON ◯ JOEY RAHIMI ◯ LUKE SKURMAN ◯
The College Prowler™ Team

Table of Contents

Introduction from the Author

Ad Majorem Dei Gloriam: For the Greater Glory of God. As I sat in my freshman orientation group, listening as every word of this Latin phrase was picked apart and thrown repeatedly against my eardrums, I began to wonder why I had chosen to make Loyola University my home for the next four years. It certainly wasn't for the greater glory of God. Maybe for the greater glory of Me, but that's a different story. As it turns out, Ad Majorem Dei Gloriam is the Jesuit motto. What I know now, four years later, is that this motto enters into every facet of life at Loyola.

My university is an extremely religious one, at least by modern standards. Sure, there are plenty of the atheists you'll find at other institutions, but they are not as prevalent here as those who believe. The fervor of the believers is thick in the air, weighing on everything years of public school had led me to believe was not a religious matter. It's not just the Catholics who run Loyola who believe, however. Faiths from all over the world are represented on campus. Hindus, Muslims, Jews, Taoists, and probably even a couple Scientologists make Loyola hum with a burning faith and conviction.

I am not talking about the "no meat on Fridays during Lent" type of faith, although the dining halls are strangely heavy on fish during that holiest part of the Catholic year. The faith I speak of is the sort of feeling that emanates from a large body of people intent on success. Loyola breeds confidence, and the confidence sparks a sort of excitement evident in even the most sleep deprived of undergraduates. For Loyolans, God is not just a concept, God exists. He is not a sort of vague, spiritual entity. God is in the books. God is in the classroom. God is in the very chalk on the board. God is learning, and students gather daily to worship at his altar.

Now, I would hate to give the impression that Loyola is rife with religious fanatics. It is not. The point I am driving at here is quite different from that. The Jesuit credo, originally meant to reference works done in the name of the Almighty, lends itself to a different cause here. One might say "For the Greater Glory of Scholarship!" has become Loyola's new battle cry. Chicago's Jesuit institution is a bastion of knowledge in the middle of an urban jungle. Students and faculty alike work hard to promote learning in everything they do. Loyola may not have the reputation of schools like Harvard or Yale, but it offers the youth it aims to teach a chance to enter into an environment where mental and personal growth reign supreme.

Undergraduates often wander into Loyola's fold confused. Many had hoped to go to another school but settled for Loyola in the end. Some just did not know what else to do with their post-high school lives. Whatever their backgrounds may be, students leave Loyola as men and women, well prepared to face the challenges of the world before them. Not sure if you're ready to go through the good and the bad of Loyola? Maybe a quick look at some of the pages here enclosed will help you decide.

Nathan Ramin, Author
Loyola University Chicago

By the Numbers

General Information
Loyola University Chicago

Lakeshore Campus
6525 N Sheridan Rd.
Chicago, Illinois 60626

Water Tower Campus
820 N. Michigan Ave.
Chicago, Illinois 60611

Control:
Private

Academic Calendar:
Semester

Religious Affiliation:
Roman Catholic (Jesuit)

Founded:
1870

Website:
www.luc.edu

Main Phone:
(773) 274-3000

Admissions Phone:
(312) 915-6500, or toll-free at
(800) 262-2373

Student Body

**Full-Time
Undergraduates:**
6,592

**Part-Time
Undergraduates:**
1,324

**Full-Time Male
Undergraduates:**
2,684

**Full-Time Female
Undergraduates:**
5,232

Admissions

Overall Acceptance Rate:
82%

**Early Decision
Acceptance Rate:**
N/A

Regular Acceptance Rate:
82%

Total Applicants:
11,009

Total Acceptances:
9,078

Freshman Enrollment:
1,915

**Yield
(% of admitted students
who actually enroll):**
21.0%

Early Decision Available?
No

Early Action Available?
No

Regular Decision Deadline:
Rolling

**Regular Decision
Notification:**
N/A

Must-Reply-By Date:
May 1

**Common Application
Accepted?**
No

Supplemental Forms?
Yes

Admissions Phone:
(312) 915-6500, or toll-free at
(800) 262-2373

Admissions E-mail:
admission@luc.edu

Admissions Website:
www.luc.edu/admission

**First Year Students
Submitting SAT Scores:**
36%

SAT I or ACT Required?
Either

**SAT I Range
(25th – 75th Percentile):**
1050-1270

**SAT I Verbal Range
(25th – 75th Percentile):**
540-640

**SAT I Math Range
(25th – 75th Percentile):**
510-630

Retention Rate:
84%

**Top 10% of
High School Class:**
28%

Application Fee:
$25

SAT II Requirements:
None

**Transfer Applications
Received:**
1,448

**Transfer Applicants
Accepted:**
1,216

**Transfer Applicants
Enrolled:**
591

**Transfer Applicant
Acceptance Rate:**
83.9%

Financial Information

Full-Time Tuition:
$22,484

Room and Board:
$8,850

Books and Supplies for class:
$800

**Average Need-Based
Financial Aid Package:**
$20,488
(including loans, work-study,
grants, and other sources)

**Students Who
Applied For Financial Aid:**
96%

Students Who Received Aid:
76%

Financial Aid Forms Deadline:
N/A

Financial Aid Phone:
(773) 508-3177

Financial Aid E-mail:
lufinaid@luc.edu

Financial Aid Website:
www.luc.edu/finaid

Academics

The Lowdown On...
Academics

Degrees Awarded:
Certificate
Bachelor's
Post-bachelor's certificate
Master's
Post-master's certificate
First professional
Doctorate

**Most Popular
Areas of Study:**
22% Business
12% Social sciences
11% Biology
11% Psychology
7% Nursing

Graduation Rates:
Four year:46%

Five year: 66%
Six Year: 69%

Full-Time Faculty:
940

**Faculty with
Terminal Degree:**
98%

→

Student-to-Faculty Ratio:
13:1

Average Course Load:
Five Classes

Undergraduate Schools:
College of Arts and Sciences
School of Business Administration
School of Education
The Marcella Niehoff School of Nursing
School of Professional Studies
School of Social WorkCollege of Engineering
College of General Studies

Special Degree Options
Accelerated Master's Programs: Five year B.S./M.A. programs in Computer Science, Criminal Justice, Math, Political Science, Psychology-Applied Human Perception and Performance, Psychology-Applied Social Psychology

Dual Degree Programs: Physics and Computer Science, Math and Computer Science, Physics and Engineering

AP Test Score Requirements
Possible credit for scores of 4 or 5

IB Test Score Requirements
Possible credit for scores of 6 or 7

Did You Know?

Fun Facts:

- Loyola's 1963 NCAA champion basketball squad was the first major Division I college team to play **four African Americans** among its starting five.

- Loyola is home to one of the larger **Jesuit communities** in the world, with 100 priests, brothers, and scholastics all serving the university and its surrounding area in some way.

- Loyola's football team was dubbed the "Ramblers" in 1926 because it **traveled constantly** throughout the United States. Although the football program was discontinued in 1930, the unique Rambler name remains.

- The movie **Flatliners,** starring Kiefer Sutherland, was filmed primarily at Loyola's Lakeshore Campus.

Best Places to Study

Cudahy Library

Jesuit Residence Lawn

Carton's Diner (Water Tower Campus)

Students Speak Out On...
Academics

> **"There are plenty of good teachers and classes to be had, but the best way to avoid the bad ones is to get advice from RAs and friends."**

Q "**The teachers, in general, are qualified** and bring knowledge and enthusiasm about the subjects to the classroom."

Q "There are **some good and some bad teachers,** like any college. Harvene Mann, who teaches Women in Literature and other similar courses, is a wonderful, fascinating teacher. I would highly recommend her classes to anyone. The books she chooses and the way she handles them makes for a really good class."

Q "Generally, I found the teachers to be very engaging. Obviously, there are a few exceptions, but **most classes were taught by full profs,** not just grad students, who were genuinely interested in what the students were doing. They were very accessible outside of classroom hours for projects that didn't always relate directly to the material. More than one prof, for example, read and gave poignant feedback on editorials I was writing for the student newspaper."

Q "A lot of universities have faculty that focus a great deal more on their own research, but Loyola's professors possess, above all other career motivations, **an immense desire to teach,** not only on their area of specialization, but also other valuable life lessons and skills."

Q "It seems like there are more good profs than bad, but it's a big school, so there is a little of both. The one good thing about Loyola is that **the grapevine will keep you informed** as to which professors are good and which are not."

Q "I was in an honors natural science class and by the end I felt like I wanted to be a botanist. It was thoroughly engaging, fun, and comprehensive, and my professor thoroughly enjoyed the topic he was teaching. Conversely, I took a physical science class where the teacher had clearly been teaching from the same lesson plan for the last ten years. **It was dry, uninteresting,** and despite taking meticulous notes and extra studying, I still was only able to get a B in the class because of curve balls thrown at us on the tests."

Q "Loyola has teachers you will want to become, and **teachers you will want to behead.** The trick for me is not to be intimidated or overly skeptical about the fact that you may have a Jesuit priest as your professor, because Jesuit priests are smart as all get out. And some have been kicked out of the Catholic Church before, indicating they're rebels, willing to smite tradition in favor of social justice."

Q "In general, **the professors at Loyola were very good**. I found most of them easily accessible and motivated to perform well."

Q "I knew students who babysat for their professors' kids, who had **beers with their professors** after class, who knew their prof's office hours by heart, and called them by their first names. If it got any more intimate, we'd all be going to class naked."

The College Prowler Take On...
Academics

Although there is certainly disagreement on the topic, most students agree that the best thing about studying at Loyola is the amount of care professors put into teaching their classes. Few teachers live on or even near campus, but this does not stop them from going out of their way to meet outside of their class schedule with students who require assistance. This relationship benefits both sides by creating a strong community of learning where students turn into instructors and instructors become students. Unfortunately, because of constant budget cuts, it is sometimes impossible for professors to provide their students with the materials necessary for learning. Further, the elimination of some of a department's programs severely hinders its ability to recruit students. Recently, Loyola's financial situation has stabalized somewhat, allowing for improvement of the academic environment.

With the sad financial state of the university in mind, it is still possible to find nationally acclaimed programs at Loyola. The business school has a record of excellence, providing many men and women the background and environment they need to be successful in the fast paced climate of a big city's economy. Graduates from all of Loyola's departments leave with a strong sense of social justice. Many of them find homes providing aid in various forms to communities throughout the world. Anyone looking to pursue a pre-medical or pre-law degree at Loyola will find the school superbly equipped to answer to their needs, both in facilities and in professional assistance. In the end, although he or she may have to deal with more administrative red tape the average academic, any student with a desire to learn can excel in any department at Loyola.

The College Prowler™ Grade on
Academics: B-

A high Academics grade generally indicates that professors are knowledgeable, accessible, and genuinely interested in their students' welfare. Other determining factors include class size, how well professors communicate, and whether or not classes are engaging.

Local Atmosphere

The Lowdown On...
Local Atmosphere

Region:
Midwest

City, State:
Chicago, Illinois

Setting:
Third largest city in America

Distance from Detroit:
4.5 Hours

Distance from St. Louis: 4.5 Hours

Points of Interest:
The Art Institute of Chicago
The John G. Shedd Aquarium
The Field Museum
The Sears Tower
The Hancock Building
Wrigley Field
Soldier Field
U.S. Cellular Field
The United Center
Tribune Building
Wrigley Building
The Magnificent Mile (Michigan Avenue)
The Loop
Grant Park
The Lakeshore
The Adler Planetarium
Museum of Science and Industry
Terra Museum
DuSable Museum of African American History
Museum of Contemporary Art
The Picasso (at the Daley Plaza)
Navy Pier
Cadillac Theater
House of Blues

Closest Shopping Districts:
Magnificent Mile, Belmont Ave., North Ave., Davis St. (Evanston)

Closest Movie Theatres:
Lakeshore Campus:
Village North Theater
6746 N. Sheridan Rd.
Chicago, IL 60626
(773) 764-9100

Century 12 Evanston
1715 Maple Ave.
Evanston, IL 60201
(847) 492-0123

Water Tower Campus:
600 N. Michigan Ave.
Chicago, IL 60611
(312) 255-9347

Esquire 6
58 E. Oak St.
Chicago, IL 60611
(312) 280-1205

AMC River East 21
322 E. Illinois St.
Chicago, IL 60611
(847) 765-7262

Navy Pier IMAX 1
600 E. Grand Ave. Ste 115
Chicago, IL 60611
(312) 595-5629

Major Sports Teams:
Cubs (baseball)
White Sox (baseball)
Bears (football)
Bulls (basketball)
Blackhawks (hockey)
Fire (soccer)

Did You Know?

5 Fun Facts about Chicago:

- While Chicago is known as a **great baseball town,** its two teams have had a difficult time becoming world champions. The White Sox last won it all in 1917, and the Cubs' World Series drought stretched to 95 years after their recent loss in the National League Championship Series to the Florida Marlins.

- Chicagoans are split on how their town received its title of the "Windy City." Many prefer to chalk it up to the **blustery weather** blown in off of Lake Michigan. Others, however, remember an old story about the propensity of local politicians to be full of hot air.

- Chicago is home to 2,896,016 people (according to the 2000 census), making it the **third most populous** in America behind Los Angeles and New York City.

- Standing at an imposing 1,450 feet and 110 stories high, Chicago's Sears Tower is the **tallest building** in North America.

- The Art Institute of Chicago holds the largest collection of **impressionist paintings** outside of Paris, including a large selection of Monets and Gauguins.

Famous Chicagoans:

Jane Addams	Louis Farrakhan
John Belushi	Chris Farley
Andre Braugher	Harrison Ford
Dick Butkus	Benny Goodman
Al Capone	George Halas
Chris Chelios	Dorothy Hamill
Michael Crichton	Herbie Hancock
John Cusack	Rickey Henderson
Clarence Darrow	Marilu Henner
Walt Disney	Hugh Hefner

Famous Chicagoans
(*Cont'd...*)**:**

Kenny Lofton

Bernie Mac

David Mamet

Curtis Mayfield

Jenny McCarthy

Mr. T

Bill Murray

"Baby Face" Nelson

Eliot Ness

Bob Newhart (Loyola alum)

Aidan Quinn

Lou Rawls

Pat Sajak

Shel Silverstein

Gene Siskel

Mel Torme

Robert Townsend

Antoine Walker

Raquel Welsh

Kayne West

George Wendt

Robin Williams

Local Slang

Sweetness: Bears legend Walter Payton

MJ: Bulls icon Michael Jordan

The El: The famous elevated train system

The Loop: Chicago's downtown area, surrounded by the El

Cheeseheads: Wisconsinites

LSD: Lakeshore Drive

The Friendly Confines: Wrigley Field

"Cheesborger, cheesborger": What to order at Billy Goat Tavern

Da Coach, Iron Mike: Famous former Bears coach Mike Ditka

The Dan Ryan: The section of I 90/94 that runs through city

Downstate: Anywhere in Illinois south of Chicago

The Eisenhower Expressway, the Ike: I 290 Expressway

The Taste: The Taste of Chicago, a large summertime festival

The Magnificent Mile: Michigan Avenue south of LSD and north of the Chicago River

Metra: Railroad service that helps suburbanites get in and out

Second City, Chi-town: Nicknames for Chicago

Stoop: Stairs in front of a house

Students Speak Out On...
Local Atmosphere

{ "Chicago is a fantastic city with plenty of other schools in town. There is plenty to do and see in Chicago: museums, sporting events, parks, architecture, etc. Just stay away from Cabrini Green."

Q "What can be said about Chicago that hasn't already been said? It's one of the best cities in the world. There is plenty of culture, music, bars, attractions, etc. to keep you busy. **Northwestern and DePaul aren't too far away,** so there are thousands of college students in the city. Unfortunately, with Chicago being the third largest city in the country, there are plenty of places to avoid. Check with the police department or the campus security about neighborhoods to avoid."

Q "**Chicago is an unbelievable town** to live in, with so much to do and see. There are plenty of universities, but don't expect to recognize college students from the other millions of people in the city. You'll doubtlessly visit the Mag Mile at some point, go to the Field Museum at least once, the Art Institute several (free on Tuesdays!), and Grant Park on a nice, sunny day. No need to be ultra touristy and check out the Sears Tower; in the end, it's just another big building."

Q "**Chicago is the city for twenty-one and older,** so you'll be spending your time drinking in your dorm/apartment anxiously waiting for your 21st birthday. It's a lot of waiting. We don't like to talk about the other universities present in Chicago—they are inherently evil."

Q "There is something for everyone in Chicago. **There are other colleges and universities around**, but they don't interact to that great of an extent."

Q "Simply, Chicago rocks. That was the reason I came to Loyola. I live in a huge city, one that keeps the same Midwestern traditions I grew up with, and didn't feel too intimidated in. As such, there are plenty of other universities around—DePaul, the University of Chicago, and Northwestern, most notably, but there are smaller schools like the University of Illinois-Chicago as well. **Any real Loyola student hits up the Cubs games** as often as possible."

Q "Chicago has so many neighborhoods! It's really up to you to decide which ones you like. Rogers Park specifically has a more residential feel to it, and you can get a really nice apartment for relatively cheap rent. **I would avoid the Jarvis Red Line stop** after dark."

Q "Remember to take some classes downtown at the Water Tower campus. It's located on some of the most expensive real estate in the city of Chicago, directly adjacent to the Magnificent Mile, and **the views from the classrooms are spectacular**. It also gets you out into the heart of the city; many Lake Shore campus students have the tendency to become too parochial, remaining in Rogers Park instead of getting out to see the sights."

Q "Loyola is in Chicago, not Boulder and not Madison. There's crime. There are bums. **There are cars on fire in the alleys.** If you want a college town, complete with lax liquor laws, Animal House antics and townspeople who wear your school's colors and shout, "Go Wildcats!" or whatever, go somewhere else."

Q "**Get a travel guide.** Even in 4 years you probably won't see it all."

The College Prowler Take On...
Local Atmosphere

That last quote pretty much sums it up: it is next to impossible to become bored in Chicago unless you try really, really hard. Chicago is the heart and soul of the Midwest. The Second City pulses with the combined energy of an entire region. The first thing a student must know is that Chicago is likely much larger than anywhere he or she has ever lived before. As intimidating as this idea can be, Chicago manages to remain friendly and inviting to those unused to its hustle and bustle. Because many Chicagoans have migrated to the city from other places, most are willing to help outsiders find their way around the many highlights and lowlights of the place they call home.

One of the things that makes Chicago so accommodating to students is that, in many ways, it is just one big college town. In addition to Loyola, Chicago features DePaul University, University of Chicago, University of Illinois in Chicago, Northwestern, Columbia College, Illinois Institute of Technology, and many other minor schools. Odds are that many of the people you see walking the streets are enrolled in one university or other. This overall community of youthful exuberance makes for an exciting city life. Street festivals happen so often during the summertime it seems like the city is hosting one big, never-ending party. The Chicago Blues Festival, Taste of Chicago, Venetian Nights, and many other fairs attract thousands to the city. Winter is the time for the thriving European community to shine, with Oktoberfest and the Kristkindlemakt highlighting a surprisingly eventful time of year.

A-

The College Prowler™ Grade on

Local Atmosphere: A-

A high Local Atmosphere grade indicates that the area surrounding campus is safe and scenic. Other factors include nearby attractions, proximity to other schools, and the town's attitude toward students

Safety & Security

The Lowdown On...
Safety & Security

Number of LUC Police:
41

LUC Police Phone:
44-911 (for on-campus emergencies),
(773) 508-6039
(non-emergencies)

Safety Services:
8-RIDE student shuttle/escort service
Rape Aggression Defense System (R.A.D.) classes
Emergency Phones (Blue Light phones)

Health Services:
Basic medical services
on-site pharmaceuticals
STD screening
counseling
immunizations

Health Center

Loyola University Wellness Center

Lakeshore Campus

Campion Hall, Lower Level

1144 Loyola Ave.

Chicago, IL 60626

Telephone: (773) 508-2530

Fax: (773) 508-8790

Immunization Fax: (773) 508-2505

Hours: Monday-Thursday 8 a.m.-6 p.m., Friday 8 a.m.-4 p.m.,
Saturday 9 a.m.-1 p.m.

Did You Know?

Loyola's police force consists of a mixture of **off duty law enforcement officials** from Chicago and Cook County, as well as a number that are trained specifically for the university's needs.

Students Speak Out On...
Safety & Security

{ **"The campus is well-lit and small enough to have buildings (and people) nearby at all times. There's a sense of seclusion from the bad neighborhood around campus."**

Q "The Chicago Police Department is your best bet for security, but a constant presence they are not. The only way to stay secure and safe in this urban setting is to just be smart, keep your head about you and **always maintain an eye on your possessions**, because they'll disappear if you're not careful."

Q "On campus **they do a pretty good job** of keeping you safe."

Q "Rogers Park isn't the safest neighborhood in the world, but **I never felt unsafe on campus**. If I were walking from the north area of campus to the south, for example, I would go out of my way to make sure I went on campus paths, where the yellow emergency call boxes are located. It's a big city, so use common sense. Walking in groups, making sure there are no unescorted girls at night, so on, and you'll be fine."

Q "The campus is equipped with emergency blue-light phones scattered throughout, but that's about the best security you're gonna get. **The campus police are ineffectual;** all they're useful for is getting you written up, and for taking you to the hospital when you're sick. The heaviest artillery I've seen them carry is a Maglight, so if you're getting mugged, don't count on much help."

Q "Security and safety is, from my perspective, very good. LUC offers an escort service wherein walking or driving escorts can be provided at a student's request after dark. Obviously, in a big city like Chicago, there is no 100 percent guarantee of safety, no matter where in the city you are, or what time of day it is, but **it is very easy to learn safer routes,** and it never hurts to establish a repertoire that is conducive to not getting raped or mugged."

Q "**The area around Loyola is somewhat troublesome,** but Loyola doesn't seem to have much more crime than any other university. Being in the city, I think Loyola students pay more attention to security and tend to keep their guard up."

Q "Security and safety at Loyola is a joke. UIC, Northwestern, and DePaul employ armed off-duty police officers as their campus police. Loyola uses rent-a-cops who make minimum wage, and have little to no training. **Loyola is in a high crime area** and the campus 'police' are ineffective."

Q "The rent-a-cops have leashes tied directly to the Resident Assistants. Their time is consumed by breaking up parties and locating mysterious 'incense' smells looming in the hallways. Safety is about as good as it can get for a Chicago university. There will be muggings and theft. **They do absolutely nothing** for cars stolen off of Loyola property. Be forewarned."

The College Prowler Take On...
Safety & Security

The most troubling fact about Loyola for prospective students is that it's located in an area of Chicago that can be dangerous. While the neighborhood is getting better and is generally well patrolled by both campus and city police, new students would be well advised to keep their eyes peeled for danger when out and about in Rogers Park. Students agree that as long as you keep your wits about you, you stand a good chance of being okay on the mean streets around campus. Still, just about everybody knows at least two or three people who have been mugged, attacked, or threatened somewhere between their apartments and the university.

It must be emphasized that students must exercise caution, after dark. Until they have a sense of their area and begin to know their way around the neighborhood, students should avoid walking alone in areas they are unfamiliar with. By taking simple extra precautions, students can take control of their situation and lessen the probability that they will become victims. To the extent that it is possible, the university protects its students in every way it can. Student escort services, such as the free "8-RIDE" van, although slow on busy nights, can make a huge difference in the planning of a safe evening.

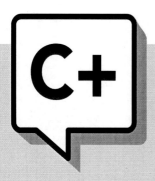

The College Prowler™ Grade on

Safety & Security: C+

A high grade in Safety & Security means that students generally feel safe, campus police are visible, blue-light phones and escort services are readily available, and safety precautions are not overly necessary.

Computers

The Lowdown On...
Computers

High-Speed Network?
Yes.

Wireless Network?
No... but there are plans for one

Number of Labs:
12, plus a few departmentally administered labs

Operating Systems:
PC
MAC

Discounted Software
None

24-Hour Labs
Mertz Hall Lab

Charge to Print?
Yes

Did You Know?

Each of Loyola's on-campus housing facilities is wired to allow **Internet access** in every room.

• Loyola is currently in the process of replacing approximately one third of its computers with **new models.**

Students Speak Out On...
Computers

{ **"The computers at the labs are adequate, though a little run down at times (keyboards that stick, faulty mice, etc.)."**

Q "Sometimes **the computer labs are rotten places to be writing,** oh say, a twenty-page thesis while someone next to you downloads stuff off Napster, instant messages their friends, talks on their cell phone, and eats Cheetos. In those cases, I would suggest getting a crappy computer for papers, and using the computer labs for the Internet and printing stuff."

Q "Computer labs are usually fairly accessible, but **I would recommend bringing your own computer."**

Q "The computers themselves are fine; Loyola does a good job updating and maintaining their infrastructure. But because of the high volume of users, **things are more often than not broken**: one machine doesn't have a working CD drive, another has a keyboard with the "shift" and "x" keys removed. Spend the extra thou and get yourself a computer for your room, so you can IM and share music like everyone else. Plus, you don't need a TV, either. You just watch DVDs on your monitor."

Q "While the location of the labs is convenient, **it is sometimes difficult to get access to a computer**, especially around finals. Oftentimes, if you do get a computer, programs do not load correctly or are absent completely from the PC, or, if you're really lucky, continually bombard you with porn pop-ups."

Q "You are paying something like $80,000 for the college education. Pay the extra grand and **bring your own computer.** It will be worth it when you don't have to shlep across campus on some cold January night to write the paper you have been putting off for weeks."

Q "**Loyola provides high speed Internet access** to all its students. Most dorm rooms are equipped with the high speed internet which makes instant messaging and downloading MP3s the two most popular campus activities."

Q "**The computer labs are plentiful,** but having your own computer is nice, especially on the cold winter nights when you don't want to walk across campus to the labs.

Q "Best advice: if you can afford it, bring your own computer and printer. **The network's fine** and you'll avoid extra hassles at the lab."

Q "Computer labs have become more crowded over the years due to the increase in enrollment, so just memorize the busy times: early in the morning when people are typing papers, lunch, and almost perpetually during exams, especially at night. Beware that each student is only **allotted a certain amount of printouts each semester,** and after that its five cents a page on your bursar bill."

The College Prowler Take On...
Computers

While many universities are becoming more and more wired, Loyola is comparatively technologically challenged. This can be good and bad. For those who are not comfortable with computers, it is completely possible to make it through most Loyola courses with only a rudimentary knowledge of a word-processing program. Anyone interested in higher-level computer systems will be disappointed. Loyola computers generally have your basics such as Internet Explorer, Microsoft Office, and so on, but anything else is not available on most systems. Many students also tell horror stories about campus computers inexplicably malfunctioning and destroying things like their forty-five-page opus about Afghani-American politics. Computer labs are great for e-mailing and reading up on the latest Bulls loss, but trying to write a paper on one is like trying to watch C-SPAN while people all around you are watching MTV. Concentration is almost impossible while everyone around you is doing something much more entertaining. Still, certain labs can be found that allow for an at least decent scholastic environment. For instance, the two located in the basement of the Crown Center are generally bastions of quiet and concentration around finals time.

The College Prowler™ Grade on
Computers: C+

A high grade in Computers designates that computer labs are available, the computer network is easily accessible, and the campus' computing technology is up-to-date.

Facilities

The Lowdown On...
Facilities

Student Center:
Centennial Forum Student
Union (CFSU)

Libraries:
5

Athletic Center:
Halas Sports Center
Alumni Gym at the Lakeshore
Campus

Popular Places to Chill:
The Ashtray
Jez Rez lawn
CFSU

What Is There to Do On Campus?

In your brief moments of free time, you can catch a game at the Gentile Center or Alumni Gym, watch a movie in Finnegan Auditorium, see a play at the Mulaney Theater, take a dip in the pool, go for a run around the track, play tennis across from the union, or take a nap under the trees planted sporadically throughout campus.

Favorite Things to Do:

One of the things Loyola students are most likely to forget about as their stay at the university lengthens is Lake Michigan. The lake is so close that it becomes just another thing to walk by on the way to class. This is unfortunate, as the lakefront is probably the best, most beautiful thing about the Lakeshore Campus. The lakefront is a great place to study, play ultimate Frisbee, check out the hot guys and girls, go for a swim, or just lay in the sun.

Movie Theatre on Campus?

No, but students can catch free second-run movies at Finnegan Auditorium on the ground floor of Damen Hall.

Bar on Campus?

No, although many students spend more time at Hamilton's Pub than in any campus building.

Coffeehouse on Campus?

Yes, one for each campus. Kaffecino is in Fordham Hall at the Lakeshore Campus; Wolf and Kettle Cafe can be found on the ground floor of Lewis Towers at the Water Tower Campus.

Students Speak Out On...
Facilities

> "Halas is a nice enough athletic center. It's no total fitness center, but for the casual exerciser, it's just fine, with yoga and dance classes offered throughout the year."

Q "If you're looking for a student center, keep heading north. You won't find one here. The facilities are still standing, which by my measurement is about as good as you can get at Loyola. **They've been renovating**, so in a few years everything should be up to par."

Q **"Facilities range from great to sub-par.** The gym is too small, and at peak hours is too crowded. If you want to use it, make sure to have an alternate plan for staying up late or going very, very early. If you're smart, you'll learn to start using the gym at the downtown campus, which sees much less traffic."

Q **"The student center, simply put, isn't.** It's a big area with some tables, but there's nothing really that interesting going on there. When big events happen, such as a band playing, or even things like 9/11, it's a great gathering place."

Q "Halas Sports Center is nice but small. If you're going to attend any of the group fitness classes, you have to get there early to reserve your spot, and **the classes almost always fill up.**"

Q "I suggest you plan your class schedule according to classroom location and season. **Dumbach Hall will be too hot in the summer** and too cold in the winter."

○ "The Sky Building involves massive amounts of stairs and faulty elevators. If you want classroom comfort, where you freeze in the summer and burn in the winter, **I would suggest Damen."**

○ "The facilities are rather nice. There are two new buildings being built on campus, a life science building as well as a new dorm. **There is no 'student union,'** only a lobby with some uncomfortable chairs and some tables. The computer labs have decent computers (Gateways or Dells with Pentium IIIs) and the libraries are well stocked with books."

○ "When the weather is nice **people congregate outside** Mertz Hall or on the lawn of the Jesuit Residence by the lake. But there's not much in the way of an actual student union."

○ "**The campus buildings are adequate,** and once in the upper track of a major, you'll be spending most of your time in one specific building, so you'll learn it in and out."

○ "Centennial Forum is the closest thing Loyola has to a student union building, and even that is **just the lobby of a dorm."**

○ "The athletic facilities are for the most part run down and old. **The computer labs are cramped and hot.** And there really is no student center."

○ "The athletic facilities are functional but not pretty. If you go look at DePaul's, you'll think that the gym at a correctional facility is probably more friendly-looking than Loyola's, but **we do have a nice pool,** and they just put in a bunch more exercise machines and televisions for the workout rooms."

The College Prowler Take On...
Facilities

Loyola is not a big, rich, state-run university. Therefore, you probably will not find many of the standard college amenities, such as fraternity houses, student unions, and an adequate athletic playing field, that you have been expecting. Loyola's student union exists in name only. In reality, it is little more than a lobby with some tables and an information desk. Each of the buildings that hold classes has its own little quirks—Damen looks like something out of a sci-fi movie, Sky's elevators never work, Dumbach has no air conditioning, and so on. The gyms are tiny and crowded; the wait times for some exercise machines can stretch for hours. Halas Field is little more than a lawn with a track around it. Thankfully, the sod is finally starting to take hold after years of trouble. That all changes, however, come rugby season, when Loyola's rapacious players leave gaping, muddy wounds in the greenish grass.

The plus side is that the swimming pool is quite nice, and most of the equipment at Halas and Alumni gyms is brand new. The new outdoor track, only three years old, is magnificent, although it is only 300 meters, shorter than the standard 400. Loyola's baseball and soccer teams do have access to their respective types of fields, although they are not anywhere near the university. Aesthetically speaking, Loyola's buildings on both campuses, with a few notable exceptions, are architecturally magnificent. Many students cite the ivy covered red brick walls of Dumbach and Cudahy Halls as main factors in their decision to come to Loyola. The university simply has an inviting look to it, something that marks it as a tranquil haven in the middle of bustling city life.

B-

The College Prowler™ Grade on

Facilities: B-

A high Facilities grade indicates that the campus is aesthetically pleasing and well-maintained; facilities are state-of-the-art, and libraries are exceptional. Other determining factors include the quality of both athletic and student centers and an abundance of things to do on campus.

Campus Dining

The Lowdown On...
Campus Dining

Freshman Meal Plan Requirement?
Yes

Meal Plan Average Cost:
$2,100

Places to Grab a Bite with Your Meal Plan
Lakeshore Campus:
Damen Cart
Location: Damen Hall
Food: Energy bars, chips, candy
Favorite Dish: Boxed egg salad sandwiches
Hours: 8:00 a.m. – 2:30 p.m.

Lakeshore Dining
Location: Mertz Hall
Food: All you can eat buffet
Favorite Dish: Omelets
Hours: Monday – Friday 11:30 a.m. – 1:30 p.m., 5 p.m. – 7 p.m.; Saturday – Sunday 9:00 a.m. – 1:30 a.m., 4:30 p.m. – 7:00 p.m.

Rambler Room
Location: Centennial Forum Student Union, Mertz Hall
Food: Grill, Deli, Salad Bar
Favorite Dish: Egg, ham and cheese breakfast croissant
Hours: Monday – Thursday 7:30 a.m. – 1:00 a.m., Friday 7:30 a.m. – 3:00 p.m., closed Saturday, Sunday 6 p.m. – 1 a.m.

→

Simpson Dining Hall
Location: Simpson Living and Learning Center
Food: Grill, Deli, Pasta, Salad Bar, Smoothies
Favorite Dish: Macaroni and Cheese
Hours: Monday – Thursday 7:30 a.m. – 10:00 p.m., Friday – Sunday 7:30 a.m. – 7:00 p.m.

Union Station
Location: Centennial Forum Student Union, Mertz Hall
Food: Convenience Store with frozen pizzas, ice cream, Ramen noodles, etc.
Favorite Dish: Bagel Dogs (like corn dogs, but better)
Hours: Monday – Thursday 7 a.m. – 12 a.m., Friday 7 a.m. – 10 p.m., Saturday – Sunday 10:00 a.m. – 10:30 p.m.

Water Tower Campus 25 East Pearson Street Internet Cafe
Location: 25 E. Pearson St. Building
Food: Snacks, Deli, boxed sandwiches
Favorite Dish: Energy Bars
Hours: Monday – Thursday 7:00 a.m. – 9:00 p.m., Friday – Saturday 7 a.m. – 5 p.m., closed Sunday

Off-Campus Places to Use Your Meal Plan:
None

24-Hour On-Campus Eating?
No

Student Favorites:
Simpson Dining

Other Options:
A Subway and Kaffecino Coffee Shop are located on the ground floor of Fordham Hall at the LSC. A new Chipolte is minutes away from campus.

Did You Know?

Looking for some mealtime entertainment? For various holidays, student organizations will occasionally **hire bands,** ranging from mariachi to reggae, to play in Rambler room during meal times. New televisions installed in the dining halls show music videos and news programs.

Students Speak Out On...
Campus Dining

{ **"Campus food is so-so. The Simpson dining room is good, Rambler room is good, and Lakeshore Dining Hall is horrible, but it's an all you can eat buffet—quantity over quality."**

Q "The food on campus is doable, though not exactly cheap. Dining at one of the residence halls costs roughly the same as it would cost to eat at a fast-food restaurant. Even so, it's probably a good idea to **go with a minimal dining plan** and add money onto it later if need be, as your balance is not rolled over at the end of the semester."

Q "Don't expect to avoid the 'freshman fifteen,' even if you only hit the salad bar. **None of the fare offered can be considered health food**. Avoid Lakeshore Dining at all costs, except for brunch on Saturdays and Sundays. Wolf and Kettle at Water Tower is a good snack stop."

Q "Only go to Lake Shore Dining if you feel like Loyola is ripping you off. **The food is horrible**, but since it is served buffet style, get plate after plate after plate and build an enormous food statue. Then proceed to throw it out."

Q "The food is adequate, **nothing to write home about.**"

Q "For quantity, Lakeshore Dining in Mertz Hall is your best bet with the **one-low-rate-for-unlimited-'food' setup;** for quality, head south on campus to Simpson's dining hall, and fork over for each item."

Q "If you want to pay for it, you can get decent food. I said decent, not great. The Lake Shore Dining Hall is for the iron stomachs only; the all-you-can-eat for something like $7.50 can push many over the edge. But it's a great place for breakfast, where sometimes they have fresh omelets made to order. Otherwise, hit up Simpson Hall. **The a-la-carte menu can be hard on the meal plan**, but it's generally better food: salads, a grill, a Mexican bar, waffles, a sandwich spot and an ice cream/smoothie bar. Not too bad."

Q "The dining halls have changed a lot since I was a freshman. Lake Shore Dining Hall gives you a lot of mediocre food for a flat fee. The **Rambler Room always has fried stuff**, and their rotating menu is sometimes really good. Simpson Dining Hall is pretty consistently edible."

Q "The food on campus must be good, considering **I gained fifteen pounds** my first semester, and my vegan friends didn't starve. There are many things that only need to be tried once to be understood, but there were a few staples that were okay as daily fare, like the salad bar, the bottled fruit smoothies, humus, bagels, and packages of sushi that actually won't kill you."

Q **"The food is best accompanied by cheese dip**. Pour it on everything and anything. Simpson Dining Hall is by far the best option on campus for food. You can get your fair share of grease, meat, veggie, and pizza here. They also have gummy bears, which automatically boosts them into an entirely different level."

The College Prowler Take On...
Campus Dining

It could be worse. That seems to be the attitude most students have about Loyola's on-campus dining options. This doesn't sound like the greatest endorsement, but every university receives mixed reviews about its campus dining options. Cafeteria food is pretty much universal in its quality, but Loyola does try to mix it up a little bit. Vegetarian and vegan options are always available, and the university goes out of its way to bring in various ethnic foods. One day you'll find burritos, the next humus and pitas will be on the menu, and the day after that there will be chicken curry. While the Loyola dining experience is certainly not a veritable cornucopia of culinary excellence, it could be far worse.

Which brings me to one of the primary complaints about Loyola's campus dining services: for all its attempts at diversity, the university does not have its meal plan system set up so students can use it anywhere except in the dining halls and the two on-campus coffee shops. Most schools will have a program set up with local fast food establishments or family owned businesses allowing students to use their campus cards to pay for food. This is not the case at Loyola. It is Aramark catering or nothing for students on a meal plan. Also, Loyola's Jesuit tradition compels it to make all red meat products unavailable on Fridays during Lent. This is just fine for the practicing Catholics among the student body, but they are the minority in the midst of a vibrant, multi-cultured, religious community. Another problem is the infamous Lakeshore Dining Hall. Unless you are a true believer in all-you-can-eat buffets, LSD will be sure to turn your stomach inside out for lunch and dinner.

The College Prowler™ Grade on
Campus Dining: C

Our grade on Campus Dining addresses the quality of both school-owned dining halls and independent on-campus restaurants as well as the price, availability, and variety of food.

Off-Campus Dining

The Lowdown On...
Off-Campus Dining

Restaurant Prowler:
Popular Places to Eat!

Chicago is a gourmet's dream! Because the city is chock full of establishments begging to sate your appetite, we'll focus here on restaurants closest to Loyola's two main campuses.

Lakeshore Campus:
A.J.'s Grill
Food: International Grill: burritos, gyros, burgers, hot dogs, etc.
Address: 4406 N. Broadway St., Rogers Park
Phone: (773) 508-5050
Cool Features: This late night, primarily take out establishment, also has two big screen televisions
Price: $7 and under per person
Hours: 24 hours a day, 7 days a week

Café Suron
Food: Persian
Address: 1146 W. Pratt Ave., Rogers Park
Phone: (773) 465-6500
Fax: (773) 465-5118
Cool Features: Lush interior, flamenco dancing on the weekends
Price: $20 and under per person
Hours: Tuesday-Sunday noon – 10 p.m., closed Monday

Carmen's Pizza
Food: Italian
Address: 6568 N. Sheridan Rd., Rogers Park
Phone: (773) 465-1700
Fax: (773) 465-5257
Cool Features: Chicago Style deep-dish pizza, Italian Beef sandwiches
Price: $15 and under per person
Hours: Monday-Thursday 11 a.m. – 11 p.m., Friday-Saturday 11 a.m. – Midnight, Sunday Noon – 11 p.m.

Chase Café
Food: Contemporary American
Address: 7301 N. Sheridan Rd., Rogers Park
Phone: (773) 245-0399
Cool Features: Set in a 1920s hotel lobby
Price: $12 and under per person
Hours: Monday-Friday 5 p.m. – 2 a.m., Saturday-Sunday 10 a.m. – 2 a.m.

Deluxe Diner
Food: Standard American diner
Address: 6349 N. Clark St., Rogers Park
Phone: (773) 743-8244
Cool Features: Retro interior, excellent skillet eggs.
Price: $8 and under per person
Hours: 24 hours a day, 7 days a week

Ennui
Food: Scones, muffins, bagels, and other coffee house food
Address: 6981 N. Sheridan Rd., Rogers Park
Phone: (773) 973-2233
Cool Features: Weekly live music and poetry readings
Price: $5 and under per person
Hours: Sunday-Thursday 10 a.m. – 11 p.m., Friday-Saturday 10 a.m. – 1 a.m., closed Monday

Ethiopian Diamond Restaurant and Lounge
Food: Ethiopian
Address: 6120 N. Broadway St., Rogers Park
Phone: (773) 338-6100
Fax: (773) 338-6293
Cool Features: Live jazz music Friday evenings from 6:30 – 10:30
Price: $15 and under per person
Hours: Monday-Thursday Noon – 10:30, Friday Noon – 10:30 p.m., Saturday-Sunday 11:00 a.m. – 11:30 p.m.

Giordano's

Food: Italian
Address: 6836 N. Sheridan Rd., Rogers Park
Phone: (773) 262-1313
Cool Features: Chain specializes in Chicago style stuffed pizza
Price: $12 and under per person
Hours: Sunday-Saturday, 11 a.m. – Midnight

Great Wall Chinese Restaurant

Food: Chinese
Address: 6748 N. Sheridan Rd., Rogers Park
Phone: (773) 465-5815
Cool Features: Loyola Student special includes entrée, side of rice, and an egg roll for under $5
Price: $7 and under per person
Hours: Sunday-Saturday 11:30 a.m. – 11:30 p.m.

Heartland Café

Food: American Traditional, with a focus on Vegetarian
Address: 7000 N. Glenwood Ave., Rogers Park
Phone: (773) 465-8005
Fax: (773) 465-6663
Cool Features: Loyola's student radio station does a weekly show called "Live from the Heartland," broadcasted directly from the café.
Price: $10 and under per person
Hours: Monday-Thursday 7 a.m. – 10 p.m., 7 a.m. – 11 p.m. Friday, 8 a.m. – 11 p.m. Saturday, 8 a.m. – 10 p.m.

J.B. Alberto's Pizza

Food: Pizza
Address: 1324 W. Morse Ave., Rogers Park
Phone: (773) 338-7117
Cool Features: The Giant pizza, in all of its humongous, greasy glory, will be more than enough for any student gathering.
Price: $5 and under per person
Hours: Monday-Thursday 4 p.m.-midnight, Friday-Saturday 4 p.m.-2a.m., Sunday 3 p.m.-midnight

Kashmir Restaurant

Food: Indian/Pakistani
Address: 2954 W. Devon Ave., Rogers Park
Phone: (773) 761-5751
Fax: N/A
Cool Features: Cozy interior makes for an intimate dining experience
Price: $17 and under per person
Hours: Sunday-Thursday 11:30 a.m.-10 p.m., Friday-Saturday 11:30 a.m.-11 p.m.

Leona's

Food: Italian
Address: 6935 N. Sheridan Rd., Rogers Park
Phone: (773) 764-5757
Cool Features: Live piano music
Price: $12 and under per person
Hours: Monday-Thursday 11:30 a.m. – 11:00 p.m., Friday-Saturday 11:30 a.m. – 12:30 a.m., Sunday 10:30 a.m. – 10:30 p.m.

Panini Panini Café House
Food: Sandwiches, soups, salads, coffee house fare
Address: 6764 N. Sheridan Rd., Rogers Park
Phone: (773) 761-7775
Cool Features: Patio
Price: $7 and under per person
Hours: Sunday-Saturday 11 a.m. – Midnight

Rocky's Tacos
Food: Mexican
Address: 7043 N. Clark St., Rogers Park
Phone: (773) 274-4555
Cool Features: Awesome authentic Mexican chow
Price: $8 and under per person
Hours: Sunday-Saturday 9 a.m. – 9 p.m.

Siam Pasta
Food: Thai
Address: 7416 N. Western Ave.
Phone: (773) 274-0579
Cool Features: Delivery option
Price: $7 and under per person
Hours: Monday-Thursday 11 a.m. – 10 p.m., Friday-Saturday Noon – 9:30 p.m., Closed Sunday

Standees
Food: Standard diner fare
Address: 1133 W. Granville Ave., Rogers Park
Phone: (773) 743-5013
Cool Features: Outstanding malts and shakes, made fresh to order. Try the Reuben.
Price: $10 and under per person
Hours: 24 hours a day, 7 days a week

Taqueria Las Nuevas Margaritas
Food: Mexican
Address: 1412 1/2 W. Morse Ave., Rogers Park
Phone: (773) 338-4730
Cool Features: Steps from Lake Michigan
Price: $8 and under per person
Hours: Sunday-Saturday 10 a.m. – 8 p.m.

Thai Spice Restaurant
Food: Thai
Address: 1320 W. Devon Ave., Rogers Park
Phone: (773) 973-0504
Cool Features: In addition to regular, sit down tables, Thai Spice also offers tables with kneelers so one can eat in the traditional Thai fashion.
Price: $10 and under per person
Hours: Wednesday-Monday, 5 p.m. – 10 p.m., closed Tuesday

Villa Palermo
Food: Italian
Address: 2154 W. Devon Ave., Rogers Park
Phone: (773) 465-5400
Fax: (773) 465-2855
Cool Features: Great prices for catering campus events
Price: $12 and under per person
Hours: Sunday-Thursday 4 p.m. – 1 a.m., Friday-Saturday 4 p.m. – 2 a.m.

Water Tower Campus:
Amarit
Food: Thai
Address: 1 E. Delaware Pl.,
Gold Coast
Phone: (312) 649-0500
Cool Features: Full bar stocked
with imported beers
Price: $8 and under per person
Hours: Sunday-Thursday 11
a.m. – 10 p.m., Friday-Saturday
11 a.m. – 11 p.m.

Bistro 110
Food: French
Address: 110 E. Pearson St.,
Gold Coast
Phone: (312) 266-3110
Fax: (312) 266-3116
Cool Features: Extensive,
expensive wine list
Price: $30 and under per
person
Hours: Monday-Wednesday
11:30 a.m. – 10:00 p.m.,
Thursday-Saturday 11:30 a.m.
– 11:00 p.m., Sunday 11 a.m.
– 10 p.m.

Café Luciano's
Food: Italian
Address: 871 N. Rush St., Gold
Coast
Phone: (312) 266-1414
Fax: (312) 266-1192
Cool Features: Offers three
dining rooms and a cigar bar.
Price: $30 and under per
person
Hours: Monday-Thursday 11:30
a.m. – 10:00 p.m.,
Friday-Saturday 11:30 a.m.
– 11:00 p.m., Sunday 4 p.m.
– 10 p.m.

Carton's
Food: American Traditional
Address: 21 E. Chestnut St.,
Gold Coast
Phone: (312) 664-5512
Cool Features: Serves
breakfast, lunch, and dinner at
all hours of the day
Price: $15 and under per
person
Hours: Sunday-Saturday 6 a.m.
– Midnight

Cheesecake Factory
Food: Contemporary American
Address: 875 N. Michigan Ave.,
Magnificent Mile
Phone: (312) 337-1101
Fax: (312) 337-1149
Cool Features: Thirty-
four different varieties of
cheesecake are offered.
Price: $20 and under per
person
Hours: Monday-Thursday 11:00
a.m. – 11:30 p.m.,
Friday-Saturday 11:00 a.m.
– 12:30 a.m., Sunday 10:00
a.m. – 11:30 p.m.

Downtown Dogs
Food: Fast Food
Address: 804 N. Rush St., Gold
Coast
Phone: (312) 951-5141
Fax: (312) 664-9509
Cool Features: Good carryout
within steps from the Chicago
red line stop near campus
Price: $8 and under per person
Hours: Sunday - Thursday 11:
00 a.m. - 9:00 a.m., Friday-
Saturday
11:00 a.m. - 11:00 p.m.

Flapjaws Café
Food: Bar Food, Pizza
Address: 22 E. Pearson St., Gold Coast
Phone: (312) 642-4848
Cool Features: Right across the street from Loyola's WTC
Price: $8 and under per person
Hours: Monday-Friday 11 a.m. – 12 a.m., 11 a.m. – 11 p.m. Saturday; Closed Sunday

Grillers Café
Food: Contemporary American
Address: 40 E. Pearson St., Gold Coast
Phone: (312) 274-0363
Cool Features: Daily specials include gyros and tacos.
Price: $8 and under per person
Hours: Monday-Friday 6:30 a.m. – 9:00 p.m., Saturday 9:00 a.m. – 8:30 p.m., Sunday 9 a.m. – 7 p.m.

Gino's Pizzeria
Food: Pizza
Address: 940 N. Rush St., Gold Coast
Phone: (312) 337-7726
Cool Features: A sign at the door tells you that there is no writing allowed on the mirrors or tables. The rest of the place, however, is yours to cover in graffiti. Price: $15 and under per person
Hours: Monday-Friday 12 p.m. – 2 a.m., Saturday 12 p.m. – 3 a.m., Sunday 12 p.m. – 1 a.m.

Jia's
Food: Chinese
Address: 901 N. State St., Gold Coast
Phone: (312) 642-0626
Cool Features: Dishes made as spicy or as mild as you could possibly want them.
Price: $10 and under per person
Hours: Monday-Friday 11:30 a.m. – 10:30 p.m., Saturday 4 p.m. – 11 p.m., Sunday 4:00 p.m. – 10:30 p.m.

Johnny Rockets
Food: Traditional American
Address: 901 N. Rush St., Gold Coast
Phone: (312) 337-3900
Cool Features: Try the "All American" meal at this '50s style burger joint: hamburger, fries, and a coke, followed by a slice of apple pie a la mode.
Price: $8 and under per person
Hours: Sunday-Thursday 7 a.m. – 11 p.m., Friday and Saturday 7 a.m. – 1 a.m.

Lo Cal Locale
Food: Vegetarian
Address: 912 N. Rush St., Gold Coast
Phone: (312) 943-9060
Fax: (773) 486-4344
Cool Features: Frozen yogurt flavors include angel food cake and peanut butter.
Price: $8 and under per person
Hours: Sunday-Thursday 11 a.m. – 10 p.m., Friday-Saturday 11 a.m. – 11 p.m.

Papa Milano's
Food: Italian
Address: 951 N. State St., Gold Coast
Phone: (312) 787-3710
Fax: (312) 787-3715
Cool Features: Patio open during the summer
Price: $20 and under per person
Hours: Monday-Thursday 11:30 a.m. – 10:30 p.m., Friday 11:30 a.m. – 11:30 p.m., Saturday 12:00 p.m. – 11:30 p.m., Sunday 12:00 p.m. – 10:30 p.m.

Zoom Kitchen
Food: Traditional American
Address: 923 N. Rush St., Gold Coast
Phone: (312) 440-3500
Fax: (312) 440-3505
Cool Features: Great view from the outdoor seating on busy Rush Street during the summer.
Price: $8 and under per person
Hours: Sunday 11 a.m. – 8 p.m., Monday-Saturday 11:00 a.m. – 9:30 p.m.

Student Favorites:
Carmen's Pizza
Thai Spice
Leona's

Best Pizza:
Giordano's
Villa Palermo

Best Asian:
Thai Spice
Amarit

Best Breakfast:
Deluxe Diner
Standees

Best Wings:
McGee's
Hamilton's Pub
(see listings in Nightlife section)

Best Burger:
Moody's Pub (see listing in Nightlife section)

Best Healthy:
Lo Cal Locale
Panini Panini
Jia's

Best Place to Take Your Parents:
Leona's
Carmen's
Cheesecake Factory

Did You Know?

Fun Facts:

What is Chicago-style pizza? A **deep dish pie,** deeper than any dish you've ever imagined, stuffed with cheese and whatever toppings you want, and then smothered in thick tomato sauce. The key here is that the tomato sauce is on top of the cheese.

Students Speak Out On...
Off-Campus Dining

> "The restaurants off campus are below average. Why doesn't Carmen's stay open later? Or serve decent food? At least Jimmy Johns and Papa John's are there now."

Q "As far as coffee houses go, Ennui is a good neighborhood stop, though the hip place to be is Chase Cafe. **They have open mic nights** and a massage parlor! Best coffee shop in the city is Pick Me Up, off the Addison El stop."

Q "**Restaurants off campus are mostly family-owned** (though not necessarily themed 'family restaurant'), and are relatively inexpensive, though not quite at Taco Bell prices. There's a marked lack of fast food in Rogers Park, though that is rumored to be changing."

Q "Moody's has **the best burgers** and best beer!"

Q "Like everyone else, you'll end up eating Carmen's pretty often. Mondays they have a pizza and pasta buffet that's not too bad, as long as you don't load up on the stuffed crust pizza. **You'll wise up eventually and stay away from the overpriced Leona's**. For all sorts of good times drinking food, hit up the greasy spoon twenty-four-hour diner Standee's just south of campus. It's not bad for what you get, and, if you can stand to do it, the chili cheese omelet is killer."

Q "**The crown jewel of dine-in is Moody's**, off the Thorndale stop, two south of campus. Best burgers you'll ever have, and pitchers of good, dark beer."

Q "There are tons of good restaurants in the city. Lakeview has a lot to offer as far as mid-priced, good restaurants. Off the Belmont stop, Clark's is open twenty-four hours. And **there's a burrito place off the Addison stop that's open really late**. Some of my favorite places to eat in the neighborhood are: Moody's Pub, The Heartland Café, Ennui Café, Deluxe Diner, and you can get really good Indian food anywhere on West Devon."

Q "Due to the cost of tuition, **I couldn't afford to eat.**"

Q "Be prepared to get on the El train to find any good restaurants. Once you do that, the world is your deep-dish pizza, as it were. **Chicago is the best eating city in the world**, I think, but Loyola's neighborhood, Rogers Park, somehow got left out of the pie. I actually would beg you to avoid all near-campus eating spots, and instead get off at Belmont, Fullerton, Argyle, or Chicago on the Red Line, and eat your face off."

Q "Off campus food is terrific. Hamilton's has food specials every night. **Giordano's has the best deep-dish Chicago-style pizza around.** Get the stuffed cheese and spinach; you'll thank me later. Leona's has excellent food in a casual atmosphere. Downtown has the best restaurants in the world, though they are pricey. Evanston has a variety of unique eating experiences."

Q "Standees, at the corner of Granville and Broadway, is a Loyola tradition, with its twenty-four hours of diner food, coffee, and jukebox tunes. It's the quintessential diner experience. **Leona's is a good place to take your parents** for regular American fare, though Café Suron right next to White Hen on Pratt is the best food, and best value, around. Panini Panini is a great sandwich spot, and the Heartland Café, right off the Morse Red Line stop, is a great new age café (ultra vegetarian)."

The College Prowler Take On...
Off-Campus Dining

Which restaurant is the most popular in Chicago? The question is impossible to answer. The city is packed with some of the finest eateries in the world. Overall, Chicagoans love big, hearty dinners, so you won't have that much success finding lighter fare. Don't worry about it! One of the most important things for a person new to Chicago to do is enjoy the food. So buy some pants with an elastic waistband and pig out. Windy City cuisine shines most in its many ethnically diverse neighborhoods. Devon Avenue is home to a bevy of Indian and Middle Eastern restaurants. If you're looking for Mexican, go north on Clark Street. Crave Chinese? Get off the Red Line at 35th Street. If you want it, you can find it in Chicago.

Some students would point out that none of the best restaurants in the city are located near Loyola's main campus. This is not entirely true. While Rogers Park is not as wealthy in fine dining as some other Chicago neighborhoods, students should certainly explore their local options. Nearly all of the restaurants near the Lakeshore Campus are family owned and serve great food. Each one has something great to offer: Carmen's has the best buffet near campus, Giordano's has some of the best deep-dish pizza in Chicago, Great Wall offers the most food for the least amount of money, and so on. To top it off, all but a few fit right into a student's tight budget. If you find yourself somehow displeased with all the restaurants in Loyola's area, go to another neighborhood. You'll find something you like, guaranteed.

The College Prowler™ Grade on

Off-Campus
Dining: A

A high off-campus dining grade implies that off-campus restaurants are affordable, accessible, and worth visiting. Other factors include the variety of cuisine and the availability of alternative options (vegetarian, vegan, Kosher, etc.).

Campus Housing

The Lowdown On...
Campus Housing

Room Types:

Residence Hall rooms at Loyola can roughly be divided by the number of students they hold. Standard room types are singles, doubles, triples, and quads. In addition, Simpson Living and Learning Center has suite style rooms, consisting of two or three double rooms situated around a common area and a bathroom.

Students in Singles:
8%

Students in Doubles:
52%

Students in Triples:
1%

Students in Apartments:
39%

Best Dorms:
Campion Hall
Creighton Hall
Simpson Living and Learning
Center
Fordham Hall

Worst Dorms:
Coffey Hall
Mertz Hall

Dormitories
Campion Hall
Floors: 3
Total Occupancy: About 150
Bathrooms: Shared by Floor
Coed: Yes
Percentage of First-Year
Students: 100%
Room Types: Doubles
Special Features: Campion
Hall has been designated as
a "quiet hall," meaning that,
at least theoretically, strict
measures are taken to ensure
the best study environment for
first-year students. Holds TV
and study lounges, and opens
up onto an enclosed courtyard.

Coffey Hall
Floors: 4 + basement
Total Occupancy: More than
200
Bathrooms: Shared by Floor
Coed: No
Percentage Men/Women:
0%/100%
Percentage of First-Year
Students: 100%
Room Types: Doubles

Coffey Hall (*Continued...*)
Special Features: Coffey Hall is
Loyola's only single-sex dorm,
housing female students along
with a contingent of nuns. Each
room is wired for the internet
and has its own sink. The
ground floor houses a large
conference room.

Creighton Hall
Floors: 7
Total Occupancy: 116
Bathrooms: In Room
Coed: Yes
Percentage of First-Year
Students: 100%
Room Types: Doubles and
Triples
Special Features: Creighton
Hall is newly refurbished. In it
you'll find a recreation area, a
laundry room, and internet and
cable access.

Mertz Hall
Floors: 19 + basement
Total Occupancy: More than
600
Bathrooms: Shared by Floor
Coed: Yes, by floor
Percentage of First-Year
Students: 100%
Room Types: Singles, Doubles
Special Features: Mertz Hall
is the largest building in the
neighborhood of Rogers Park.
Two computer labs, wired for
the internet, two dining halls,
TV and study lounges, and
beautiful views of Rogers Park
and Lake Michigan. Located
above Centennial Forum
Student Union.

Simpson Living and Learning Center

Floors: 5
Total Occupancy: More than 400
Bathrooms: Shared by Suite
Coed: Yes
Percentage of First-Year Students: 100%
Room Types: Singles and Doubles arranged as Suites
Special Features: Study and TV lounges, kitchenettes, and laundry facilities on each floor. The ground floor houses a computer lab, a mail facility, and the finest dining hall on campus.

Apartment-Style Halls

Fairfield Hall

Floors: 4
Total Occupancy: More than 200
Bathrooms: In Room
Co-Ed: Yes
Percentage of First-Year Students: 0%
Room Types: One bedroom Triples and two bedroom Quads
Special Features: Typical rooms hold one or two bedrooms, a bathroom, a kitchen, and a living room.

Holy Cross Hall

Floors: 6
Total Occupancy: More than 100
Bathrooms: In Room
Co-Ed: Yes
Percentage of First-Year

Holy Cross Hall (*Continued...*)

Students: 0%
Room Types: Doubles and Triples
Special Features: Each room is full carpeted with a kitchen, bathroom, and living room.

Rockhurst Hall

Floors: 5
Total Occupancy: More than 100
Bathrooms: In Room
Co-Ed: Yes
Percentage of First-Year Students: 0%
Room Types: Studio Doubles, One Bedroom Triples
Special Features: Ground floor houses the main office for all apartments on the south end of campus. Apartments have a kitchen, private bath, carpeting and air conditioning. Triples feature balconies.

Saint Louis Hall

Floors: It is divided into two, five-story buildings
Total Occupancy: 170
Bathrooms: In Room
Co-Ed: Yes
Percentage of First-Year Students: 0%
Room Types: Studio Doubles, one-bedroom Triples, and two-bedroom Quads
Special Features: Each room holds its own kitchen and bathroom.

Santa Clara Hall

Floors: 9

Total Occupancy: 220

Bathrooms: In Room

Co-Ed: Yes

Percentage of First-Year
Students: 0%

Room Types: Singles, Doubles,
Triples, and Quads

Special Features: Study area,
TV lounge, and laundry room
on ground floor. Spectacular
views of Lake Michigan from
most rooms. Next door to the
beach.

Seattle Hall

Floors: 4

Total Occupancy: 60

Bathrooms: In Room

Co-Ed: Yes

Percentage of First-Year
Students: 0%

Room Types: Triples and
Doubles

Special Features: Seattle Hall
houses the largest rooms on
campus, each equipped with
kitchens and new appliances. A
parking lot is available for the
use of residents.

Xavier Hall

Floors: 5

Total Occupancy: 72

Bathrooms: In Room

Co-Ed: Yes

Percentage of First-Year
Students: 0%

Room Types: Studio Doubles
and one-bedroom Triples

Special Features: Offers
parking beneath the building
to residents. Kitchens and
bathrooms in every room.

Fordham Hall

Floors: 16

Total Occupancy: 350

Bathrooms: In Room

Co-Ed: Yes

Percentage of First-Year
Students: 0%

Room Types: Doubles and
Quads

Special Features: Residence
restricted to third and fourth
year students. Apartments on
east side of building provide
panoramic views of the
Lakeshore Campus and Lake
Michigan.

Undergrads on Campus:

29%

Bed Type
Twin extra long beds can be arranged either as bunks, singles, or lofts.

Available for Rent
Mini refrigerators

Cleaning Service?
Dormitory common areas are cleaned by staff approximately every other day during the week

What You Get
Bed, desk, chair, bookshelf, dresser, closet, Ethernet connections, free campus calls.

Also Available:
Loyola provides dormitories designated as "quiet halls" for those students who are concerned that the college party scene could hinder their study habits.

Did You Know?

- All campus housing at Loyola is now **smoke free.**

- Many of Loyola's residence halls have been **recently renamed.** With that in mind, it can be good to get to know both the old and the new names of many buildings, as they are often referred to by both.

- Loyola requires all students with less than fifty-six credit hours to **live on-campus.** That means most people will have to wait until after sophomore year to find their dream apartment off campus.

- Coffey Hall is Loyola's only **single-sex dorm.** The rest hold to about the same pattern of 63% female, 37% male.

Students Speak Out On...
Campus Housing

"Don't try to own a rabbit, put marshmallow Peeps in the microwave, or feed the 'girl who doesn't drink' ten shots of vodka, or you'll have to spend a lot of time explaining to your RA why you're such a troublemaker."

Q "Your best friends are going to be the people you lived near your first year, so **hope to God you don't get the dorm with the nuns**. They've changed the names of all the other halls in order to confuse people like me who might give you wise advice, so all I know is that the one that was once called Lakefront, now Santa Clara Hall, is the place to be."

Q "Having spent my freshman year in Simpson, I'm partial to it, but **I also like the added measure of privacy** you have there; the rooms are set up as suites, with two or three two-person rooms sharing a bathroom. If you have a good relationship with the suitemates, it's a great way to live. "

Q "If you're more for the communal, typical college dorm experience, Mertz is the way to go. It's set up in a large square, with the rooms along the outside, the elevators and stairs in the middle, and four bathrooms for the whole floor. The drawback? Don't live there if you don't enjoy walking down many flights of stairs on many occasions, many times in the cold, since some jokester hit the fire alarm. **The upperclassman apartments aren't too shabby;** go Santa Clara or Fordham Halls for some quality living."

Q "The dorms are pretty good, with some structured like typical dorms (one to two communal bathrooms per floor of residents), and **some more modern and private** (rooms divided into suites wherein four to six students share one, semi-private bath). Naturally I will plug Simpson Living & Learning Center, as I chose to live there over Mertz, and really liked the set-up of suites and non-massively-communal bathrooms."

Q "Both Simpson and Mertz, the two main dormitories on campus, **allow for you to never leave the building** (except to go to class), as they have computer labs, dining halls, study lounges, and recreation areas all under one roof (Mertz, being connected to the student union, has much more going on its building), which is a really good thing during the winter."

Q "Any dorms that I would suggest to avoid have, fortunately, been torn down in the past two years, so **no worries.**"

Q "Simpson is nice. In Mertz you get to walk down **as many as nineteen floors** when someone pulls the fire alarm."

Q "Mertz people will say it's better, but they're wrong. **Go Simpson!**"

Q "As far as freshman dorms go, Simpson and Campion draw about an even overall quality. **Simpson has coed floors and private bathrooms** for every three rooms, but is usually the preferred dorm, and hard to get into. Mertz, though the victim of frequent fire alarms, is truly nineteen floors of fun. Each floor by year's end has its own identity, for people bond quickly due to the ordeal of living there. The motto of Mertz is 'Mertz 'till it hurts!'—but I loved it."

Q "The dorms are about average, though better than most state schools. Simpson is nicer than Mertz, but Mertz is usually more active. Avoid Mertz if walking down ten flights of stairs in the middle of the night doesn't appeal to you. Many students, with enough liquid courage, like to pull the fire alarms. The new dorm under construction across from Simpson looks great, and **Granada Center is the nicest** of the upperclassmen dorms."

Q "The dorm rooms are extremely nice, which was one of the major draws to Loyola. Simpson Living Learning Center has the newest rooms. The biggest rooms on campus can be located here, as well as the smallest dorm rooms. If you want mice for company, then Mertz is the place to go. If you're lucky enough to get a corner room **you'll have an awesome view of Lake Michigan.** The downside is that females and males are separated by floor, whereas Simpson allows both genders to run rampant on the same floor."

The College Prowler Take On...
Campus Housing

Like most other universities, Loyola requires freshmen to live in on-campus dormitories. This may not sound like a blast, but sharing a communal bathroom and living under the tyrannical boot of an RA can be the perfect bonding experience for young men and women who have not lived away from home before. Most students agree: the people you live with freshmen year will probably be some of your best friends four years later. Even if your roommate is a nightmarish slob, or a stuck up neat freak, odds are you'll be able to find dozens of people you can relate to within the walls of your residence hall. The time you spend packed into a dormitory with hundreds of other vibrantly individual people will be one you look back on and relish.

Although the standard cry of Mertz Hall residents is "Mertz 'til it Hurts!" don't let all those people who live in Simpson or Campion get you down. If you choose to live in Mertz Hall, yes, you will have to deal with fire alarms in the middle of the night during finals, a laundry room with more broken machines than functional ones, and elevators that only work on the third Tuesday of every month, but you will also live in what is arguably the social center of campus along with about 500 other people. You could certainly do a lot worse than Mertz. You could live in Coffey Hall. Known as the "Virgin Vault," the most distinguishing feature of Coffey is that it frustrates both young men and women. The guys can't get in, and the girls can't get them in. Simpson's rooms are clean, but rather small. Each room holds two people and is arranged with two or three other rooms into a suite. Kept at such close quarters, students cannot help but get to know their suite-mates quite intimately.

B

The College Prowler™ Grade on

Campus Housing: B

A high Campus Housing grade indicates that dorms are clean, well-maintained, and spacious. Other determining factors include variety of dorms, proximity to classes, and social atmosphere.

Off-Campus Housing

The Lowdown On...
Off-Campus Housing

Undergrads in Off-Campus Housing:
71%

Average Rent for a Studio:
In Rogers Park: $450/month

In the Gold Coast: $800/month

In Lincoln Park: $600/month

Average Rent for a 1BR:
In Rogers Park: $650/month

In the Gold Coast: $1,000/month

In Lincoln Park: $800/month

Average Rent for a 2BR:
In Rogers Park: $900/month

In the Gold Coast: $1,600/month

In Lincoln Park: $1,200/month

Popular Areas:

In Rogers Park, Northshore Avenue, Albion Street, Arthur Street, Columbia Street, and Loyola Avenue are all popular among students. Further away from campus, students can be found in Wrigleyville, Lincoln Park, Edgewater, and Lakeview. The Gold Coast and the Loop are outside of most students' price ranges.

Best Time to Look for a Place:

Start of second semester

For Assistance Contact:

Loyola does not provide any apartment finding services, but it does direct students to contact one of the following services if they need assistance.

Simply Roommates and Sublets

http://www.simplyroommates.com/

Phone: (773) 755-4400

Just Passing Through

http://www.justpassingthrough.com

Phone: (312) 501-3310

Students Speak Out On...
Off-Campus Housing

"Off-campus housing is plentiful. Most apartments are converted houses and rent for $2000-$3000 a month. With 4-6 people per apartment the rent is cheaper than the dorms."

Q "It is definitely worth it to get off campus. **Freedom from the dorm is wonderful**, though be aware that you can still receive disciplinary action for having a party within a four block radius of the Loyola campus. So, if you live north of Pratt, you're safe. Just know you'll be walking four blocks in the dead of Chicago winter."

Q "You can't live off campus until your junior year, which is funny because they don't have enough housing for everyone. So you're stuck picking a random lottery number in hopes they can locate a place for you to live. All of which could be avoided if they allowed sophomores to live off campus. **Off-campus housing is relatively cheap,** and Resident Advisor free. I strongly recommend it."

Q "**Housing is very convenient;** the whole area around the university is apartments."

Q "Starting junior year, the majority of **students elect to rent flats in brownstones** on the north side of campus; the south side offers apartments which students can also rent. It's a good idea to secure a lease early in the spring for the upcoming fall to find what you're looking for, especially if you need a flat with four or more bedrooms, as those are few and far between."

Q "The search effort is worth it, because living off campus allows for much more freedom than living on campus, and **off-campus housing is much, much cheaper."**

Q "Three words: get off campus. Dollar for dollar, it's cheaper, in both room and board, than living on campus. But be aware: many landlords in the Rogers Park area know their buildings are going to be rented by college students, and don't care to keep them up, but then again, they don't care if you host parties and damage the place either. **It's really easy to find a place,** as there are plenty of listings in The Reader, Chicago's free weekly paper, or just walk up and down streets, looking for the 'for rent' signs. It's worth it."

Q "Live off campus your sophomore year if at all possible! The rent in Rogers Park is so much cheaper than living on campus. And **there are tons of cute apartments** within walking distance of Loyola."

Q "Housing off campus is easy to find and pretty cheap. **Definitely do your research** to make sure you're not getting a 'fixer-upper-opportunity.'"

Q "Yes, the housing is worth it. **Get the heck out of the dorms** and start actually having fun at Loyola. This is when it all begins. The dorms are okay freshman year because you need a safe haven while you get used to Chicago and all that it entails, but after that, by all means, get one of the cheap flats around Rogers Park with three or four friends and start throwing parties and living life."

Q "Be careful not to get in a situation when **you'll have to sublease to someone else** because it always sounds like it'll be easy when it actually will be murder."

The College Prowler Take On...
Off-Campus Housing

One thing Loyola students complain most about is the requirement that they live on campus for their first two years. Not only is the housing off campus much cheaper, it's generally nicer and often better administered. The only thing students have to watch out for is the propensity of certain local landlords to take advantage of students. The greater majority treat their student tenants like they would any other, but some tend to overcharge for rent and disappear when the radiators start leaking all over the floorboards. With this in mind, there are all kinds of housing options for students in Chicago. Most are large three or four bedroom flats running for about $1,500 to $1,700 a month.

It's not difficult to find housing by Loyola's Lakeshore Campus, but there are also many other neighborhoods in Chicago for students who don't mind a bit of a commute to explore. An apartment in Old Town or Streeterville can be quite expensive, but if you're a business student taking most of your classes at the Water Tower Campus, this is an option you may want to look into, as Loyola does not have a dorm downtown. Edgewater is a developing area south of Rogers Park offering inexpensive housing not too far from campus. Wrigleyville is a popular destination for Loyola seniors, as it is not that far from either campus via the Red Line train, plus it places students within walking distance of Wrigley Field and many neighborhood bars. Lincoln Park is a little bit pricy, but it offers a beautiful, growing environment close to DePaul University where students can get a taste of another university's nightlife. As long as you are careful when looking into your housing options, you should be able to find a little corner of Chicago that you can call yours for a reasonable price.

The College Prowler™ Grade on
Off-Campus Housing: A-

A high grade in Off-Campus Housing indicates that apartments are of high quality, close to campus, affordable, and easy to secure.

Diversity

The Lowdown On...
Diversity

American Indian:
0%

White:
68%

Asian or Pacific Islander:
11%

International:
2%

African American:
9%

Unknown:
0%

Hispanic:
10%

Out of State:
32%

Political Activity

Most students are vaguely liberal. There is some activism on campus. Because the university sets up voting centers on campus for local, state, and federal elections, a fair amount of students register and vote. In recent years, there have been many protests over what students and faculty view as varying levels of administrative mismanagement and incompetence.

Gay Tolerance

As it is with most subgroups, the campus is quite accepting of its gay and lesbian students. Loyola's gay and lesbian organization, the Rainbow Connection, is more active than many groups around campus and has tried, with varying success, to sponsor student events. Its' predecessor, GLABA, was one of the first gay and lesbian organizations at a US private institution.

Economic Status

LUC has students from every kind of economic background. Although tuition is expensive, the university does offer a large amount of financial aid to students. Most students are neither rich nor poor, but there is a contingent from the northern suburbs of Chicago who come from fairly wealthy families.

Minority Clubs

Loyola's minority clubs are very active on campus. There is an abundance of clubs that sponsor cultural events and parties in Centennial Forum Student Union. One of the more popular events is the annual Def Comedy Jam, which always brings in a number of students.

Religion

Because it is a Jesuit university, many practicing Catholics make their way to Loyola. This does not mean Loyola does not have other religious groups however. The Jewish organization Hillel thrives on campus, and there is a quite sizeable Muslim presence as well. Although it is somewhat smaller than the others, Loyola does have something of a Hindu community also. All religious groups have been historically quite good at coming together during times of crisis. Although certain overseas events such as the Arab-Israeli conflict have played as divisive forces from time to time between groups, for the most part, Loyola's myriad religious groups practice tolerance and understanding towards one another.

Students Speak Out On...
Diversity

{ **"The campus is extremely diverse. People of all cultures attend the university and celebrate its diversity."**

Q "Loyola will claim to be diverse. It isn't. They are the only school in Chicago without an African American studies major. There are **many ethnicities, but not many people within them**. For a school in Chicago, they need to work on expanding their diversity."

Q "The diversity, **as far as viewpoints and opinions go**, is huge."

Q "There are **students from every walk of life**, and there is an organization for all of them."

Q "The campus is relatively ethnically diverse and many student organizations represent the different ethnicities, races, and nationalities that exist in the Loyola student body. The Rogers Park neighborhood, home of the Lake Shore Campus, is **very diverse in culture."**

Q "**The LSC is religiously diverse**, with a number of the major world religions represented by student organizations."

Q "As far as diversity, I'd say there are a good number of both Asian and Indian students, but it's still **predominantly white."**

Q "There are **a number of Greek ethnic organizations**, and many of the student cultural organizations hold events, such as when the Middle Eastern students serve food in the student union for all to enjoy."

Q "There are quite a few ethnic groups, but it seems like they all form clubs and keep to themselves. If you can get involved with one of those clubs it's really fun! **I had a great time hanging out with the people in BCC** (Black Culture Club)."

Q "Loyola is situated in one of the most diverse places in the world. Loyola itself has relatively large populations of Asian and Indian students, but as far as African Americans and Latinos go, there's not a great mix. But **diversity is one of the things Loyola claims it is proud of**, and if you see the list of nation-oriented student groups, you'll have to agree, although whether that fosters diversity or separatism will have to be up to you."

The College Prowler Take On...
Diversity

Although Loyola is quite proud of its perceived diversity, many students tell a different story. Many ethnicities are represented, but there are few large communities at the school. Students feel that different groups tend to keep to themselves. Loyola's lack of an African American studies major is often lamented. Still, you will hear several languages other than your native one every day, and courses that attract overseas students will be populated by a diverse student body. The neighborhood around campus is a cultural Mecca, and many students will find themselves going through something of a culture shock when they first venture out into the streets of Rogers Park.

One thing Loyola has been criticized for in recent years is its lack of a recruitment push in Chicago. A large number of students come to Loyola from Jesuit high schools in Cincinnati, St. Louis, and downstate Illinois. This makes for a mostly white, Catholic community in the middle of one of the most ethnically diverse cities in America. The African American and Latino crowds, while active on the university scene, are smaller than perhaps they could be. The university does a good job of making minorities feel welcome by providing opportunities for them to come together as groups, but it could do an even better job by focusing a little bit more of its energy on recruiting in Chicago's many ethnic neighborhoods, and thereby diversifying its student body a little further.

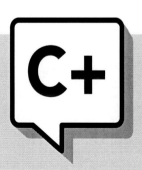

The College Prowler™ Grade on
Diversity: C+

A high grade in Diversity indicates that ethnic minorities and international students have a notable presence on campus and that students of different economic backgrounds, religious beliefs, and sexual preferences are well-represented.

Guys & Girls

The Lowdown On...
Guys & Girls

Men Undergrads:
37%

Women Undergrads:
63%

Birth Control Available?
No. As a Catholic university, Loyola does not support any kind of birth control other than abstinence.

Loyola does offer free STD screenings.

Social Scene

Pretty much everyone finds it initially difficult to start conversations when faced by the daunting task of entering the college social-scene. Any level of aloofness is quickly rendered tricky to maintain when you are thrown into dorm life however. Even students who find social interaction difficult are drawn into interacting with other students at this generally gregarious campus. It is sometimes hard to get people to branch out beyond their particular groups once they become entrenched in them.

Hookups or Relationships?

The first month or so of school will be your chance to get to know more people than you ever knew existed in the world. That said, there will be a lot of people out there looking for that special someone. Once the school year really gets rolling, however, many students begin to focus more and more on their studies, and relationships fall to the wayside. For girls, the numbers are certainly against you; all the guys may be taken by mid-November. Around finals time, everyone gets a little bit frustrated, so that may just be your lucky time of year.

Best Place to Meet Guys/Girls

Loyola is not a party school by any means, but that doesn't mean that students don't like to go out. Exhibit A to this hypothesis is Thursday night at Hamilton's pub. The otherwise only reasonably busy establishment becomes packed wall to wall with students, particularly freshmen, sophomores, and all those upperclassmen who are not yet sick of pushing their way through this human meat market. Hamilton's can be a lot of fun on any night, and an unhealthy amount of people meet their significant others there.

If the bar is just not your style, it is perfectly possible to meet people around campus. Some students just roll out of bed and go to class in their pajamas, but a large percentage dress to the nines. There are few better ways to get to know that hot girl in your biology lab than to invite her over for a pre-exam cram session. Also, most Loyola dorms are coed, so great guys and girls could be little more than a floor away from you.

Did You Know?

Top Places to Find Hotties:

- Men's and Women's Volleyball games
- Thursday nights at Hamilton's
- Halas Sports Center

Top Places to Hookup:

- Hamilton's
- The beach
- Off-campus parties
- Jez Rez Lawn
- Simpson Hall (because it's the cleanest)

Dress Code

NCAA Division I sports may not be popular at Loyola, but the student body is a fairly athletic one all the same. You see a lot of sporty looking people walking around, wearing baseball hats, soccer jerseys, and exercise pants. At the Water Tower Campus, students mostly dress business casual, with khakis, button down skirts, blouses, and skirts being standard. At the Lakeshore Campus, people like to look nice while staying comfortable. Most kids are gigantic fans of blue jeans, polo shirts, and hooded sweatshirts. Around finals time, this all changes, and slippers and sweat pants come into fashion.

Students Speak Out On...
Guys & Girls

> "The students at Loyola are all around good people. There are two girls for every guy so finding a date is never hard, if you're male."

Q "There are **two girls for every guy,** and some of them are even pretty cute."

Q "There are **lots of hotties on campus;** check out Hamilton's on a Thursday night and you'll see what I mean."

Q "Loyola guys are not frat boys, nor are they theatre geeks, machismo athletes, narcissistic trust-fund babies, or nerdy brainiacs—**all of those stereotypes**, plus a combinations of several of those stereotypes, are represented on Loyola's campus."

Q **"The girls, frankly, stink.** There are no knock-outs, but most of them act like they are. A lot of the girls have crabby, selfish personalities, and drink way too much, way too often. Most of them are teases. I'm one of them."

Q "I'm a guy . . . **darn right I'm hot**. It's no ASU, but the girls are decent."

Q "If you have patience to deal with a few annoying or obnoxious girls first, you can find a decent number of girls that are **relatively level-headed** and not over-consumed with how much money their parents make in comparison to their suite mates."

Q "You'll find something eventually. Just remember one of the best places to pick up a girl for more than a one-nighter is in class. **Keep your eyes open."**

Q "The most frequent complaint heard by the girls is that **'he's either not cute, gay, or taken.'** Most of the cute girls already have boyfriends, but I guess that's because they're cute."

Q "There are **some pretty fine looking people** at Loyola. The Lakeshore campus is cool because you meet many different kinds of people with different interests. And most of them are decent looking too."

Q "As far as the guys, a lot of them are of the Business-school-I-ironed-my-boxers-this-morning guys, a lot are **long-haired exiles from Stonerville**, a lot are really grateful that Loyola doesn't seem to care what your high school GPA was, and still more are from Asia, India, and Cincinnati. The girls, well, there's the blond, stupid girl from St. Louis, the blond, stupid girl from Oak Park, and the blond, stupid girl from Naperville. Avoid those three basic types and the rest of the girls should be fun, smart, and beautiful."

Q **"Nobody is hot,** but you'll think they are eventually anyway after a few shots at Hamilton's."

Q "The girls at Loyola are **pretty hot."**

The College Prowler Take On...
Guys & Girls

GQ is definitely not knocking down the doors to get to Loyola's guys and you won't see the girls on the cover of Cosmopolitan. Still, the campus overall is a fairly attractive one. The problem is that for most of the year, Loyola students hide their most attractive features with scarves, gloves, and long underwear. You would think that any piece of uncovered flesh would immediately turn to ice and fall off, which could theoretically happen in Chicago's frigid winter. The trick is to get people out of their cold weather clothes. Then they're hot. The best part about students is that they all come from different social and economic backgrounds, making it very likely you'll find someone to curl up by the fire and drink hot cocoa with on a cold night.

Students are not at Loyola because they wanted to have fun while at college. The university does not have the academic prestige of Harvard, nor does it challenge the party reputation of places like Indiana University. Loyola is somewhere in between. Students find a way to blend academic prowess with having a good time. Most students do not go around looking to get laid, but people can let themselves go when the right party arises.

The College Prowler™ Grade on
Guys: B-

A high grade for Guys indicates that the male population on campus is attractive, smart, friendly, and engaging, and that the school has a decent ratio of guys to girls.

The College Prowler™ Grade on
Girls: B+

A high grade for Girls not only implies that the women on campus are attractive, smart, friendly, and engaging, but also that there is a fair ratio of girls to guys.

Athletics

The Lowdown On...
Athletics

Athletic Division:
NCAA Division I

No. of Males Playing Varsity Sports:
100 (2%)

Conference:
Horizon League

No. of Females Playing Varsity Sports:
100 (1%)

Men's Varsity Sports:
Basketball
Volleyball
Golf
Soccer
Track and Field
Cross Country

Women's Varsity Sports:
Softball
Basketball
Volleyball
Soccer
Golf
Track and Field
Cross Country
Lacrosse

Club Sports:
Baseball
Cycling
Equestrian Polo
Lacrosse
Men's Rugby
Women's Rugby
Women's Soccer
Tennis
Men's Volleyball
Women's Volleyball

Intramurals:
Badminton
Basketball (three on three)
Basketball (five on five)
Chicago Style Softball
Dodgeball
Flag Football (four on four)
Flag Football (eleven on eleven)
In-Line Hockey
Inner-tube Water Polo
Kickball
Nine-Ball
Playstation 2 Tournaments
Racquetball
Soccer (indoor and outdoor)
Table Tennis
Ultimate Frisbee
Volleyball
Volleyball (four on four)
Wallyball

Athletic Fields
Halas Field
Loyola Soccer Park
Loyola Softball Park

School Mascot
Loyola's teams all go by the name Ramblers, but the school mascot is a wolf named Lou who apparently originates in Loyola's coat of arms.

Colors
Maroon and Gold

Getting Tickets

It is easy to get tickets to all of Loyola's sporting events, and they are all free to students. The only exception to this rule is when a national power such as Michigan State comes to town to play the basketball team, in which case tickets can be scarce.

Most Popular Sports

Loyola's volleyball teams are always nationally ranked and generally have a large following. The men's basketball team has flirted with respectability in recent years, and nearly made the NCAA tournament in 2001. The men's and women's club rugby teams may be the most popular draws at the university. Intramurals are incredibly popular, especially Chicago-style softball, soccer, and flag football.

Overlooked Teams

The women's softball team is consistently quite good, but their field is nowhere near campus. Crowds for the women's basketball team are notoriously sparse, even when Loyola fields a competitive team. The men's soccer team attracts few fans, but plays an up-tempo, exciting game.

Gyms/Facilities

Joseph J. Gentile Center, Lakeshore Campus

The "Joe" is where Loyola's basketball teams fight for supremacy in the Horizon League. It is a fairly new facility awkwardly situated at the center of the Lakeshore Campus.

Alumni Gym, Lakeshore Campus

The "Big Brown Box that Rocks," Alumni Gym is the former home of Loyola's basketball teams. Currently, Loyola's successful men's and women's volleyball teams play there. In addition to the main courts, the facility houses enough exercise equipment to keep LUC's student-athletes in playing shape.

Halas Sports Center, Lakeshore Campus

Halas is the main athletic facility for students at Lakeshore Campus. Inside you'll find three floors with everything you need to help take off that pesky freshman fifteen. The equipment has been renovated, but due to space constrictions is meager at best. The pool is popular among those students looking for the optimal workout. The first floor contains male and female locker rooms, a small athletic shop, and lounge area with table tennis. The bottom floor contains racquetball courts, a free weights room, a weight machine room, an aerobic room, and cardio room. The top floor of Halas provides 3 full length basketball court and indoor track. If you like to be alone with your muscles, Halas is not the place for you. It is perpetually packed with people working out or (more likely) waiting to work out.

Students Speak Out On...
Athletics

"Varsity sports are not big, sadly, and neither are IMs, although there are some that do generate a good turn out. Maybe you should be the one to lead the team!"

Q "This school is spirit deficient. The teams are ho-hum, and nobody even tries to get the student body rallied around them. **Club intramural teams are fun** to get involved with, though the draw there isn't even that huge. The rugby teams, men's and women's, are like family and are probably the coolest people on campus."

Q "Varsity sports are not big at all on campus. Only once in my academic career has our men's basketball team sold out a home game, and that was because it was LUC vs. UIC, and a good number of those tickets were sold to UIC kids. **Men's volleyball draws a consistently large crowd**, but that's probably because the guys are cute, funny, nice, and interact more with their fellow students than the other teams' players."

Q "**Intramural sports are relatively big**, especially softball and volleyball, and especially with the coed leagues. Typically the same students that participate in intramurals as freshman still participate as seniors, and not many newbies join in later on in their academic careers."

Q "IMs are the way to go. They're all sorts of good times, and, more often than not, **you'll win by forfeit** because the other team didn't show. I think they may even have an IM ultimate Frisbee team."

Q "School spirit at Loyola stinks. No one seems to care about the teams, even when the men's volleyball squad is ranked in the top ten nationally and almost beat the number one ranked team. **There's no football team**; in its place is club rugby, the players of which do more drinking than playing."

Q "Well, we don't have a football team, but **we do have rugby**. All the other sports are moderately attended by students. I'd say basketball is the most popular. Lots of people participate in IM sports, and they're pretty fun."

Q "Well, I was typically one of the fifty people who regularly went to basketball and volleyball games. Other than that, nobody really follows the sports. **Intramurals are never that big**, but always fun."

Q "Varsity sports are almost nonexistent. **There's no football team**, so Saturdays in the winter are spent at the bar watching the games. Men's basketball and the volleyball teams attract the most fans, but success seems to elude the Loyola teams. IM sports are fun and there are many teams competing in sports like softball, flag football, basketball, kickball, etc."

Q "It depends on who you talk to. There are many who support the Ramblers excessively, but then there are others who could care less about the sports programs. One of the most underrated activities at Loyola is attending volleyball matches. **Both the women's and men's team have successful programs** so it's fun to watch."

The College Prowler Take On...
Athletics

Loyola may be an NCAA Division I school, but it hardly shows. Intercollegiate athletics are about as noticeable at the university as George was when surrounded by John, Paul, and Ringo. Few students follow the teams unless a cross-town rival, such as the University of Illinois in Chicago, comes to pay a visit. Loyola's lack of a football team upsets many students who would much rather spend their Saturday afternoons sitting on stadium seats than on couch cushions. The men's basketball team has been competitive lately, but has done little on the national stage since winning the NCAA championship in 1963. The volleyball teams are viewed as a bright spot for varsity sports by many Loyolans, but even they have only an underground following when compared to teams at other schools.

In stark contrast to its varsity squads, Loyola's intramural and club teams thrive. Fueled by a sizeable population of former high school athletes, intramurals are always popular. There is nothing (well, almost nothing) that can ease fragile nerves around finals time like a good game of flag football or indoor soccer. As far as club sports go, the rugby team probably attracts more followers than any of the varsity squads. Few things can top watching your friends beat the heck out of those scions of academia from Northwestern.

The College Prowler™ Grade on
Athletics: C+

A high grade in Athletics indicates that students have school spirit, that sports programs are respected, that games are well-attended, and that intramurals are a prominent part of student life.

Nightlife

The Lowdown On...
Nightlife

Popular Nightlife Spots!

Club Crawler:

No one will mistake Chicago's club scene for those in New York and Los Angeles, especially during the bitterly cold winter months. Be forewarned, however, clubs can be quite pricey, and almost no options exist for those without the crucial number twenty-one emblazoned on their driver's licenses.

Bar Chicago
9 W. Division St.
Gold Coast
(312) 654-1120

If you're looking for a place to relive your wildest fraternity oriented dreams/nightmares, Bar Chicago is the place for you. Don't look for martinis here; slide through the crowd and grab yourself a domestic bottle or a souvenir mug of "Hooligan Juice" at the bar, then bong a beer on your way back to the dance floor for good measure. The best (or worst) part is that you can stay pretty much as late as you

Bar Chicago (Continued...)

want: the bar is open until 4 a.m. from Wednesday-Friday, and 5:30 a.m. on Saturdays. Put your name on their mailing list for the chance to win a free VIP party. $5 cover charge on Fridays and Saturdays. Find out more at www.barchicago.com.

Specials:

Thursday: $1 Miller Lite drafts, $2 well drinks, $3 Red Bull and vodka cocktails

Circus

901 W. Weed St.

Bucktown

(312) 266-1200

Stretching to 20,000 square feet in size, Circus is one of the largest clubs in Chicago. Two rooms are open to the public, but a third is available for special events and parties. Why is it called "Circus?" Because every night, side shows walk the floor, from fire breathing men to contortionists. The club recently opened a VIP section called the Bedroom, complete with beds for those too tired to dance the night away.

Specials:

Wednesday: $5 cover, old school hip-hop

Thursday-Saturday: cover varies according to event

Domaine

1045 N. Rush St.

Gold Coast

(312) 397-1045

Domaine is an outrageously expensive, deafeningly chic new club within footsteps of some of the Gold Coast's most famous restaurants. To step beyond the velvet curtains that frame the doorway to this oasis of opulence is to step into an alternate universe where the city's richest and hippest eat caviar and drink neon martinis to the beat of house music provided by live deejays.

Specials:

None. Cover varies depending on the events planned for the evening. Take a virtual tour of Domaine on the web at www. domainechicago.com.

Le Passage

937 N. Rush St.

Gold Coast

(312) 255-0022

French house music and Polynesian drinks make this dimly lit club stand out among the after hours joints in the area. Put your name on the VIP list to help avoid long lines to get in on the weekends. Le Passage is truly one of the more innovative, intriguing clubs in Chicago.

Specials:

Wednesdays: $4 food and cocktail menu

White Star Lounge

225 W. Ontario St.

Streeterville

(312) 337-8080

White Star is loud. No matter what you do inside this hip Streeterville club, you will be overwhelmed by thumping hip-hop or raucous house music. On the weekends, lines stretch around the corner. The club offers many VIP rooms and its spacious real estate allows for multi-level rooms surrounding the dance floor. White Star presents a posh experience, celebrity sightings, and on occasion, a runway fashion show. Specials: None. Cover ranges from $10 and up.

Bar Prowler:

So many places to drink, so little time. This is the classic Chicago dilemma. Really more of a "sit down and have a beer" town than a "dance the night away" metropolis, Chicago is home to some of the best places in the world to watch a game or listen to music while sipping on the occasionally perfect pint. The following are a few of the standouts nearest to Loyola's two main campuses, as well as a few other student favorites. If you want specials you would be best advised to stick to Rogers Park, Lincoln Park, and Wrigleyville. Check www.metromix.com for updated specials.

Lakeshore Campus:

Bruno and Tim's Lounge and Liquor

6562 N. Sheridan Rd.

Rogers Park

(773) 764-7900

Looking for a good dive bar? Bruno's is one of the best. Frequented by locals as well as students who stop in for a quick one before class, this bar/liquor store is a great place to watch a game if you want to hear expert commentary from about seven guys sitting at the end of the bar. Beer and booze are on the cheap here, and it's easy to get on speaking terms with the bartenders. Just a little hole in the wall, Bruno's is great for drinking a beer and hearing the recap of the Cubs game.

Specials: $2 imports

Cuneen's

1424 W. Devon Ave.

Rogers Park

Another of Rogers Park's many dive bars, Cuneen's is popular especially among the theater students at Loyola. Go there to listen to good music, drink a pitcher of beer, and play some pool.

Specials: None, but pitchers are as low as $5 and bottles go for $2.50 and up

Hamilton's Pub

6341 N. Broadway

Rogers Park

(773) 764-8133

"Hammies" is Loyola's unofficial student bar. Most students spend an unhealthy amount of their time there. Some attest to pouring more money into this newly renovated north side bar than they did into their college education. Hamilton's is a decent bar with a bright, fresh interior and all of the standard tunes on the jukebox. Plus, drinks are on the cheap side, and they've got one of the city's many great burgers.

Specials:

Monday: Dollar half pound burgers, $1.75 twenty-four ounce Bud Light drafts, $3 Margaritas

Tuesday: Dollar tacos, $2.50 Fosters pints, $3 Amaretto Stone Sours

Wednesday: Twenty cent wings, $1.75 Coors Light Bottles

Thursday: $6.50 half slab BBQ ribs, $6 domestic pitchers, $2.75 well drinks

Friday: $4.75 12-inch pizza, $2 Bud and Bud Light bottles, $3.75 Long Islands

Saturday: $3 chicken sandwich, $1.75 Icehouse bottles

Sunday: $2.50 chicken quesadillas, $9 bucket of five Miller bottles, $2.75 vodka and lemonade

Moody's Pub

5910 N. Broadway

Rogers Park

(773) 275-2696

Moody's has the best beer garden in Chicago. Period. Once you leave the dark, cave-like interior of the bar and step into this veritable Eden of booze and burgers, you'll never want to leave. Ivy covered brick walls open up unto an area charmingly set with picnic tables and oak trees, all centered gracefully around a central waterfall. If this is not enough to draw you in, Moody's has the best burger in the city, hands down. Just going for the drinks? Get a cheap pitcher of Berghoff Dark, sip sangria, or order the Moody Mama for a fruitier option.

Specials: None, but pitchers of Berghoff go for $7

The Oasis

6809 N. Sheridan Rd.

Rogers Park

(773) 973-7788

Still not done drinking when Hamilton's closes at 2 a.m.? Head north on Sheridan road and hit the "O," Loyola's favorite four o'clock bar. If you're still functioning well enough for semi-physical activity, one half of the bar holds four dart boards and a pool table, and a couple of arcade games sit near the bathrooms.

The Pumping Company

6157 N. Broadway
Rogers Park
(773) 743-7994

"P Co." is home to the famous (at least among Loyola students) Saturday night Penny Pitchers. Freshmen and seniors mix freely at this old firehouse themed bar. Deejays spin '70s, '80s, and '90s tunes all week long, and every now and then you'll catch a live band there. An outdoor beer garden rounds out the experience, with room for up to eighty-five people.

Specials:

Wednesday: $3 Pitchers

Thursday: $2 Bud bottles

Saturdays: Penny Pitchers

Water Tower Campus:

Blue Agave

1 W. Maple St.
Gold Coast
(312) 335-8900

This Mexican themed bar/restaurant slings tequila shots and all kinds of south-of-the-border beers. Enjoy standard Mexican fare with a tequila martini, or just toss back a shot followed by a spicy, but fruity, sangria chaser. During the summertime, the Maple Street patio provides a bit of cool shade.

Specials: You get chips and salsa instead of peanuts at the bar. That can count as a meal for a hungry college student!

Dublin's Bar and Grill

1030 N. State St.
Gold Coast
(312) 266-6340

In addition to being a good place to grab beer during a Bears game, Dublin's serves as yet another one of Chicago's great burger choices. Drinks aren't too expensive considering the area it's in, and the staff is pretty friendly. Plus, their kitchen is open until the wee hours of the mornin'.

Specials: None

The Hunt Club

1100 N. State St.
Gold Coast
(312) 988-7887

The Hunt Club is one of those bars that is great during the summer, but loses some of its luster in the cold winter months. The outdoor patio, which spills out onto the busy State and Rush triangle, is perfect for sipping a cocktail in the sun and watching the crowds go by. Drinks are pricier than they are in Rogers Park, but not too bad for downtown.

Specials:

Friday: $3 lemon drop shots

Saturday: $3 apple jack shots

Sundays: $15 bucket of five Miller Lites or MGDs

Pippin's Tavern

806 N. Rush St.

Gold Coast

(312) 787-5435

Slinging beers since 1949, this small local tavern also serves up popcorn and pinball to the tiny crowd that wedges its way into the bar.

Specials: None

Streeter's Tavern

50 E. Chicago Ave.

Gold Coast

(312) 944-5206

If you're looking for a bar to play games at, go to Streeter's. You'll find pool, foosball, and ping pong tables all crammed into this underground establishment.

Specials: None

The Underground Wonder Bar

10 E. Walton St.

Gold Coast

(312) 266-7761

Groove to the sweet sounds of improvised jazz while trying to find elbow space at the bar. Every now and then one of the bar's more famous patrons will step on stage and perform with the band.

Specials: None. Cover charges start at 9 p.m. $6 Sunday-Thursday, $10 Friday-Saturday

What to Do if You're Not 21

The Metro

3730 N. Clark St.

Wrigleyville

(773) 549-0203

This renovated theater is one of the best places in the city to hear live music of any sort. Get down on the floor with a tightly packed crowd of musical devotees and just breathe in the scene. The Metro helped spark the career of the Windy City's own Billy Corgan and his Smashing Pumpkins, and he has been known to stop by every now and then. Many shows are all ages, and prices range from $5-$40.

House of Blues

329 N. Dearborn St.

(312) 923-2000

Another of Chicago's premier music joints, The House of Blues is located right on the north bank of the Chicago River. All kinds of musical acts visit the HOB, from local indie bands to international sensations, from Dr. John to Pantera. Every now and then Dan Ackroyd and Jim Belushi show up for an impromptu show as the Blues Brothers. Many shows are all ages, and prices range from $10-$25.

Improv Olympic

3541 N. Clark St .

Wrigleyville

(773) 880-0199

Improv Olympic may be second only to the Second City in the famous Chicago improvisational comedy scene. This Wrigleyville club showcases teams of improv players who craft scenes spontaneously from audience suggestions. The theater is smoke free and air conditioned, with comfortable seats and few obstructed views.

Pick Me Up Café

3408 N. Clark St.

Wrigleyville

(773) 248-6613

You could call Pick Me Up Café the opposite of a bar. It's the sort of place you stay up all night and drink coffee instead of beer. Open until 3 a.m., this café is the perfect place for Loyola students to go with or without their books before their twenty-first birthday. Get a milkshake, one of many flavored cappuccinos, or a delectable turkey sandwich, and breathe in as much of the eclectic, smoky air as your lungs will allow. Don't forget to bring a couple of bucks for the jukebox.

Other Places to Check Out:

The Full Shilling

3724 N. Clark St.

Wrigleyville

(773) 248-3330

Within steps of Wrigley Field, this new bar has some of the best specials in the city. Whether stopping by after a Cubs win or making a special trip down for their fabulous tater tots, count on the Full Shilling to fill you up with food and drinks for a small price.

Specials: Monday: $1 PBR and Bud Light drafts, $3 Jack Daniels cocktails, $3.50 Jaeger bombs

Tuesday: $2 Murphy's Irish Stout and McSorley's drafts, Magner's bottles, $2.95 Irish-style meatloaf

Wednesday: $ 2 domestic and import pints, $5.99 half-slab of ribs with fries

Thursday: $2.50 Guinness, Bass, black and tan pints, $1 Miller Lite and Bud Light drafts, $1-$2 burgers

Friday: $3 Amstel Light and Heineken bottles, $2 Blue Moon and Harp pints, $5.99 all-you-can-eat fish and chips

Saturday: $2.50 Sam Adam's seasonal bottles, $3 Pilsner Urquell and Stella Artois drafts, $4.99 surf and turf dinner, $5 Miller Lite pitchers

Sunday: Half-price drinks, $4.99 corned beef and cabbage, $2.50 Miller Lite bottles, $2.75

Goose Island Brewery

3535 N. Clark St.

Wrigleyville

(773) 832-9040

Chicago's most famous local microbrew, Goose Island produces dozens of different varieties of beer. The Wrigleyville branch is baseball themed, with a larger than life mural of several Hall of Famers, none of whom played for the Cubs.

Specials:

Every Day: $3 Goose Island bottles, $1.99 appetizers from 6 p.m. – 8 p.m.

Monday: Half price appetizers

Wednesday: Open mike night, $8 pitchers

Thursday: Karaoke starting at 10 p.m., $8 pitchers

John Barleycorn's

658 W. Belden Ave.

Lincoln Park

(773) 348-8899

Barleycorn's was originally built in 1890 by an Irish immigrant. John Dillinger frequented the place in the '20s, when it stayed open as a speakeasy during Prohibition. Barleycorn's also has a Wrigleyville location that attracts a young crowd with its mammoth dance floor.

Specials:

Tuesday: $2 Sierra Nevada drafts

Thursday: $2 Guinness, black and tan pints and bottle beers, $1 chicken wing baskets

McGee's

950 W. Webster Ave.

Lincoln Park

(773) 549-8200

Especially popular with DePaul students, McGee's may have more beers on tap than any other bar in the city. Thirty different varieties await your pleasure as you watch the big game on one of dozens of flat screen TVs mounted at just about every table. Like euchre? Know what euchre is? You can play in a tournament every Monday night at McGee's.

Specials:

Monday: $6 all-you-can-eat chili, $2.50 Bud Bottles

Tuesday: Ten cent wings, $7 Bud pitchers

Wednesday: Dollar burgers, all beers $2.50

Thursday: $4 cover after 7 p.m., $1 Bud and Michelob bottles

Friday: Free pizza at midnight, $5 martinis

Rock Bottom Brewery

1 W. Grand Ave.

River North

(312) 755-9339

Originally a Colorado institution, Rock Bottom is currently challenging Goose Island's status as most popular local microbrewery. This huge establishment is frequented by a heavy after work crowd in one of Chicago's busier business neighborhoods.

Still Need More?

Kincade's

Hi Tops

Bar Louie

the Keg

Gin Mill

Raw Bar

Gingerman

Fado

Spoon

Whiskey Sky

Cubby Bear

Sovereign

Leg Room

Funk

Lakeview Links

Jack Sullivan's

Gamekeepers

O'Hagan's

Mystic Celt

Irish Oak

Smart Bar

Schuba's

Murphy's Bleachers

Sports Corner

Lion's Head

Finn McCool's

Kendall's

Student Favorites

Hamilton's Pub

The Oasis

Bruno and Tim's Lounge and Liquor

Useful Resources for Nightlife

The Chicago Reader free newspaper

Newcity magazine

Red Eye newspaper

Red Streak newspaper

UR Chicago newspaper

www.metromix.com

Bars Close At:

2 a.m. on most nights, but many are open until 3 a.m. or even 4 a.m. on Fridays and Saturdays.

Primary Areas with Nightlife:

Lincoln Park

Rush Street

Division Street

Wrigleyville

Rogers Park

Cheapest Place to Get a Drink:

The Full Shilling

Pumping Company

McGee's

Local Specialties:

The local microbrew, Goose Island.

Favorite Drinking Games:

Beer Pong

Card Games

Century Club

Quarters

Power Hour

Flip Cup

Sink the Bismarck

Organization Parties:

Loyola's many student organizations can be counted on to throw the occasional party. Most will reserve space in either Rambler Room or Centennial Forum Student Union and bring in delicious ethnic food from local restaurants. Sometimes a club will rent out a restaurant for a private party, generally only open to club members.

Frats:

See the Greek Section!

Students Speak Out On...
Nightlife

> **"There really aren't many house parties around campus and if there are, they're busted up by about 11 p.m. The bars aren't that great, but they're serviceable."**

Q "You're in Chicago. There may not be the greatest campus party scene, but you don't need it. There's always something to do, a show going on, a movie to catch, a new club to check out. If you'd like to stay home and have people over, **the house party scene is good,** but there's so much else to do."

Q "One word: Hamilton's. Nice freshman eye candy, as most of the kids in there on a given Thursday, Friday or Saturday are fresh out of high school, and can't believe they're actually in a bar. **You'll get sick of it eventually**, but it's not a bad time. When Hammie's closes at two, make the trek north to the Oasis, which is open 'till four. It's a dive, but go with your friends and play some darts or shoot some pool. Bruno's is really for regulars only, but the dorms use the attached liquor store as their main source of drink."

Q "Yeah, that's funny, parties on campus. Don't kid yourself; party in the dorms with more than, say, six people, and **you'll get an RA on you nice and fast.** Be smart and do the off-campus party scene. During the first week, the only fraternity with a house usually has some good keggers, but they get busted and can't host any more. The rest of the year, you pretty much have to know someone to get it and find out where the parties are. But it's not hard to do."

○ "**Moody's has the best burgers in the city** and an awesome beer garden in the summer, which is great for simply hanging out with friends (and drinking sangria)."

○ "Hamilton's is the most popular bar and **tends to be very crowded on Thursday nights** (Loyola's #1 going-out night), with the front bar being more bar-like, and the back bar being more club-like, complete with a soggy dance floor and insane drum-machine music."

○ "Hamilton's is the staple bar. **Sleazy and dirty** is the charm it goes for."

○ "The quality of campus parties varies by host, but for the most part, $5 gets you unlimited access to a keg and sometimes other kinds of drinks. Of course, the popularity of the party inversely correlates with the amount of beer you will get for your buck, and the 'dance areas' are usually more for making out than grinding. There is only one 'fraternity house,' and the majority of parties are at random people's flats. **Police typically break up parties before midnight** for noise issues with the non-college student neighbors."

○ "The best place to be is Bruno's, **loaded with local regulars,** a nice reprieve from the regular bar grind."

○ "Parties on campus are nonexistent, unless you can sneak a keg into the dorms. So **make some upperclassmen friends early** who'll give you the inside scoop to the off campus parties. Bars are easy. Hamilton's just got revamped to look like a trendy sports bar and is where the majority of students go on Thursdays. Oasis is up by White Hen on Pratt and is the local 'close at four a.m.' bar, where you might go if the party ended too soon."

Q **"The parties on campus do not exist**. If you have one, you will get busted and have to go on probation and attend an 'alcohol awareness' three hour seminar. If you have another one, and that is also broken up, you have to attend the same seminar again. When Loyola finally lets people live outside of campus, parties tend to occur more frequently. However, they also have the right to break up parties off campus. So, you spend your time in bars. Hamilton's and The Oasis are Rogers Park favorites. I would know. I spent four years of my college education there."

The College Prowler Take On...
Nightlife

The first thing that must be said in a summary of Chicago's nightlife is that one cannot write a summary of Chicago's nightlife. There are far too many things to see and do than can be mentioned in a few meager paragraphs. A person could live in the city their entire life, go to a new bar every week, and still not find all of the hidden gems and obvious dives. Still, this vibrant scene does not exactly reach Loyola's neighborhood. The most common bar mentioned by students is Hamilton's, simply because it is generally seen as the best of a small number of choices. In a dive bar haven such as Rogers Park, Hammies has drink specials and a dance floor. This makes it the gold standard for Loyola students. The university hardly holds any events worth attending, and there are no fraternity houses on campus. Luckily enough, nearly all of the upperclassmen live in apartments within walking distance of campus, and all of them throw parties at one time or another. Although parties at other universities are often free, students can expect to pitch in to help pay for things at Loyola's off-campus parties. Five dollars is standard for a keg party, and only on rare occasions will it be more. As a general rule, if you pay more than $5 for a cup, there better be something pretty special about the party, or you should consider finding a different one.

Thankfully, there is more to Chicago than Rogers Park. In addition to bars and clubs, the city holds more than enough theaters, coffee houses, live music venues, comedy clubs, and bowling alleys to keep you busy until you reach your twenty-first birthday. So if you get sick of ADG, go visit the baseball house, or go to a theater party, or check out the physics club kegger, or whatever group appeals to you.

The College Prowler™ Grade on
Nightlife: A-

A high grade in Nightlife indicates that there are many bars and clubs in the area that are easily accessible and affordable. Other determining factors include the number of options for the under-21 crowd and the prevalence of house parties.

Greek Life

The Lowdown On...
Greek Life

Number of Fraternities:
6

Number of Sororities:
8

Percent of Undergrad Men in Fraternities:
7%

Percent of Undergrad Women in Sororities:
5%

Fraternities on Campus:
Sigma Alpha Epsilon
Alpha Delta Gamma
Sigma Pi
Alpha Psi Lambda
Sigma Lambda Beta
Tau Kappa Epsilon

→

Sororities on Campus:

Alpha Sigma Alpha

Kappa Beta Gamma

Gamma Phi Omega

Delta Sigma Theta

Alpha Chi Omega

Delta Phi Lambda

Phi Sigma Sigma

Sigma Lambda Gamma

Other Greek Organizations

Greek Council

Interfraternity Council

Order of Omega

Pan-Hellenic Council

Did You Know?

Once a year, Sigma Alpha Epsilon hosts its annual "Paddy Murphy Night," bringing **nationally renowned musical acts** to the university for a night of music and dancing.

• Don't see the Greek organization you're looking for listed? Loyola's Greek community is a growing one, so get a group of friends together and **start your own chapter.**

Students Speak Out On...
Greek Life

"Greek life is against Loyola policy. Animal House does not exist on this campus. The entire Greek system is based on mixers at off-campus apartments until the party gets broken up."

Q "They mostly impact the Loyola scene through their **fundraising and philanthropy efforts.** It's interesting that the newer fraternities on campus—by that I mean the ones without an established tradition at Loyola—are more egalitarian and don't hold as well to the frat boy stereotype."

Q "**Greek life at Loyola sucks.** I should know; I was in a fraternity. The school doesn't support the system, so Greeks can't do anything fun like they do at real schools. All the fraternities fit into nicely defined stereotypes."

Q "Greek life has a pulse, but that's about it. There is only one frat house. One. There are a couple other Greek organizations and **they sometimes do things like throw parties,** but you wouldn't really know it unless someone told you. The people I know that did get into the Greek life, however, seemed to think it was great and the whole university revolved around them."

Q "SAE is the most active fraternity on campus, but otherwise to the college community, they exist as a relative unknown. If you have trouble breaking into the social scene, you should be all for joining one, but **don't think it'll get you any extra respect."**

Q "**Greek life is small at Loyola.** There are about ten fraternities and sororities. The Greeks do have many parties which are open to everyone. The Greek community is also involved in numerous community service projects."

Q "There is a core group of social fraternities and sororities. It's more a side note to life at Loyola than the underpinnings of it. Those that exist hold to themselves, mostly, with one fraternity holding a mixer with one sorority in a closed party, for example. **There are few open fraternity parties.**"

Q "ADG throws **fun parties.**"

Q "Greek life definitely **doesn't dominate the social scene,** but it has been making strides. It is definitely up and coming right now."

Q "If you're a boy you might be invited to a Crush Party, in which some hideous sorority girl will reveal that she wants your body, and if you're a girl, about fifteen of those hideous sorority girls will try to recruit you. **Just tell them they're hideous and run away,** or you'll be saddled with un-fun responsibility and Greek politics for four years."

The College Prowler Take On...
Greek Life

It's difficult to find anyone who says positive things about Greek life at Loyola, even the Greeks themselves. Although there are a number of new organizations that have been started within the past few years, they are finding it difficult to grow when faced with an administration that views them as a pariah to college life. After the first few weeks of school, it seems as though every fraternity and sorority goes underground for the rest of the semester until their next rush. Yes, they do some community service projects, but these get next to no notice by anyone not wearing a pin.

The community certainly is a growing one however. Although they do not have a house, Sigma Alpha Epsilon, founded in 2000, has quickly become the largest and most active fraternity on campus. By sponsoring concerts and service initiatives, SAE has helped reintroduce a certain level of positive competition with the two other most prominent frats, Alpha Delta Gamma and Sigma Pi. Although it is still the only fraternity officially allowed to display its letters at its house, ADG has been something of a disappointment in recent years, having faced a number of disciplinary actions, and being rendered practically powerless in the Loyola community. The sororities also have their ups and downs, but they do throw some very popular mixers, although you must be on the list (or attached to someone on the list) to get in. In the end, only about 12 percent of Loyola students go Greek. Those who do generally have a blast, but the many non-Greeks are generally indifferent to their presence on campus.

D+

The College Prowler™ Grade on
Greek Life: D+

A high grade in Greek Life indicates that sororities and fraternities are not only present, but also active on campus. Other determining factors include the variety of houses available and the respect the Greek community receives from the rest of the campus.

Drug Scene

The Lowdown On...
Drug Scene

Most Prevalent Drugs on Campus:

Alcohol

Caffeine

Nicotine

Marijuana

Ecstasy

Liquor-Related Referrals:

0

Liquor-Related Arrests:

15

Drug-Related Referrals:

0

Drug-Related Arrests:

23

Drug Counseling Programs

The Counseling Center
(773) 508-2740
Services: Short term counseling and group therapy, referrals service

University Ministry
(773) 508.2200
Services: Twelve step groups, retreats, individual spiritual counseling

Students Speak Out On...
Drug Scene

"Everyone knows someone. I wouldn't say it's anything of a problem or an epidemic, but it's definitely there."

Q "What can I say? People use drugs. Its mostly pot, though **ecstasy and cocaine have a place** as well. People do what they want and hang out with who they want, but if you get caught by an authority figure, you're still dealing with an illegal substance, and you're gonna get strung up."

Q "The main drugs are alcohol and nicotine. Lots of students smoke cigarettes and many drink socially. There is a good deal of pot on campus, but other drugs are not that prevalent. Be warned though, Chicago is a big city, **if you want it you can get it."**

Q "If you want it, **you can find it."**

Q "You can get **pretty much anything you would want on campus,** if you know where to look and who to ask. However, students' drug use is not prevalent, nor is it obvious to notice which kids use. Sometimes stoners, in actuality, are just lazy kids."

Q "Yes, there are drugs at Loyola. But **I couldn't call it a 'drug scene' per se.** There are drugs at every college. There are probably drugs on every city block. Let's put it this way: it's just as easy to score some drugs at Loyola as it is to avoid them altogether. And if you do score them, try not to do a bunch of them first semester, freshman year, in your dorm and then go freaking out a la some famed single-semester alumni we know."

The College Prowler Take On...
Drug Scene

Drugs, like just about everything else you could possibly want, are abundantly available in Chicago. Not many students at Loyola resort to hard-core drug use, but there are certainly those that do. Although few people will admit it, it sometimes seems like the majority of undergraduates smoke marijuana at least every now and then, if not on a regular basis. Even if they avoid the green weed, a large percentage of Loyolans spend their non-study hours indulging heavily in alcohol. In recent years, there has been a small influx of ecstasy onto campus. Overall, drug use is not prevalent, however, and students generally do not feel pressured to do drugs. No one at Loyola will shove a joint in your face and demand that you smoke it. If you choose to do drugs, it will be of your own volition. Just remember, drugs are bad, okay?

Although they tend to welcome "soft" drugs such as alcohol, nicotine, and pot, Loyola students stay away from the harder stuff. You will find few coke-heads or heroin addicts on campus. Most people who hear about the use of this sort of drug by one of their friends are utterly disappointed. Students like to have a good time, but they do not want to see their friends become the victims of rampant drug use.

The College Prowler™ Grade on

Drug Scene: B-

A high grade in the Drug Scene indicates that drugs are not a noticeable part of campus life; drug use is not visible, and no pressure to use them seems to exist.

Campus Strictness

The Lowdown On...
Campus Strictness

What Are You Most Likely to Get Caught Doing on Campus?

- Drinking underage
- Burning candles or incense
- Parking illegally
- Noise violations in the dorm
- Being on the opposite sex's floor after visiting hours
- Possession of stolen university property
- Possession of drug or alcohol paraphernalia
- Smoking marijuana
- Climbing on top of Madonna della Strada chapel
- Climbing between windows in Santa Clara Hall
- Making or using fake IDs
- Downloading copyrighted material from the internet

Students Speak Out On...
Campus Strictness

"The campus police will likely confiscate your alcohol if you are underage. If you are caught with drugs, they may call the rebal police. Repeated violations of the residence hall policies will get you thrown out of the dorms."

Q "You get caught, **you get in trouble.** If you're unfortunate you will get caught each and every time, but if you're one of the lucky ones, you can get away with anything."

Q "They'll take your alcohol, drugs, and all paraphernalia if you're not supposed to have them, and **you'll get written up for a disciplinary hearing.** Of course, if you're dealing, well, that's the CPD's jurisdiction."

Q "Consequences such as mandatory attendance at alcohol awareness seminars are strictly enforced, as are any legal ramifications for possession of legal drugs; however, **campus police are not on an active search-and-destroy mission**, so if you get caught, it was most likely you that called the attention to yourself."

Q "Since the Chicago Police Department takes care of the heavy stuff—campus police, most being off-duty CPD officers, aren't allowed to carry firearms—the **campus patrol becomes the watchdog for an administration** bent on keeping the nebulous 'Jesuit tradition' alive: this means no mixed-sex overnights, no opposite-sex members on single-sex floors and, just recently, no smoking in the dorms."

Q "Watch it around campus cops. The CPD, on the other hand, lets most everything slide. If they're called to bust your off-campus party, **they'll tell you to keep it down and leave;** they've got much more pressing issues to attend to."

Q "In the dorms **they can be totally strict,** but that depends on your RA and how stupid you are."

Q "Just be smart and **don't get caught.**"

Q "**Campus police routinely catch someone smoking pot** in their dorm. As for drinking, if they're tough on it now, then the times certainly are a' changing."

The College Prowler Take On...
Campus Strictness

Students agree that the easiest way to keep campus security from catching you in an illicit act is to be smart about it. Loyola's police force is not out to stop students from drinking in the dorms, but if a situation gets out of hand and they have to intervene, they will. By being smart about whatever they are doing, students can avoid getting written up and having to go to things like Alcohol Awareness meetings. Chicago police also will go out of their way not to bust students engaged in liquid revelry. They have much more important things to do in Chicago, such as save people's lives, than haul a bunch of drunken college students off to jail for the night. The first time they come to your house they'll likely just tell you to keep the noise down. If things appear to be out of hand, or if they return to the party more than once in a night, only then will the CPD break up a party and begin to think about arresting people.

Resident Assistants can be a constant thorn in student's sides. RAs theoretically exist to watch over new students and provide assistance in times of emergency. Unfortunately, there seem to be an abundance at Loyola who believe their job is to seek out every minor infraction perpetrated by students, and prosecute it to the fullest degree of the university's bylaws. The university does not make it easy on its RAs, of course, forbidding them to go to student-thrown parties on or off campus. Many students find themselves tip-toeing through their halls in order to avoid getting cited for a noise violation. In an ideal world, Loyola would place more trust in the ability of its undergraduates to act as adults.

The College Prowler™ Grade on
Campus
Strictness: D+

A high Campus Strictness grade implies an overall lenient atmosphere; police and RAs are fairly tolerant, and the administration's rules are flexible.

Parking

The Lowdown On...
Parking

Student Parking Lot?
Yes

Freshman Allowed to Park?
Yes

Approximate Parking Permit Cost: $190.50 per semester, $381 for the whole academic year

LUC Parking Services:
Department of Public Safety
Parking Office
508-2403
www.luc.edu/depts/safety/
parking.html

Parking Permits:
It is possible for undergrads to get parking permits, but most go to commuters.
You can purchase a pass online to save time.
For city parking, purchase permits from the alderman's office, thereby avoiding the hefty $75 fine.

➜

Best Places to Find a Parking Spot:

Before 5 p.m. on Arthur, Northshore, Albion, and Columbia streets

Good Luck Getting a Parking Spot Here:

Chicago. Seriously though, it will be difficult to find parking anywhere in the city. At the Lakeshore Campus, it is toughest to park south of campus. It is impossible to park at the Water Tower Campus without paying an arm and a leg.

Common Parking Tickets:

Expired Meter: No meters on campus

No Parking Zone: $30.00

Handicapped Zone: $100.00

Fire Lane: $100.00

Parking Without a Permit: $45.00

Parking in the Wrong Zone: $45.00

Students Speak Out On...
Parking

> **"If you're bringing a car, be prepared to pay hefty garage fees, or $100 for a Chicago city and zone sticker. I recommend the city sticker, although parking is limited on the streets."**

"You don't need a car. **Parking does not exist** in Chicago."

"Parking stinks. It's expensive and **your car might not be there in the morning.** The public transit and the shuttle buses eliminate the need for a car unless you absolutely need it."

"**Don't bring a car,** you don't need one. Parking is a pain, or expensive, or both."

"Students can park in several lots, or the main parking structure on campus with the possession of a semester pass or daily fee, respectively. **Parking in the main garage is rarely difficult**, and street parking, with either a Chicago City Sticker or daily permit for that particular zone, is relatively easy on some of the north side. However, further north where more students live per block, it becomes more difficult after 5 p.m. Street parking on the south side of campus is virtually impossible."

"**Parking on campus is good**; there is a parking garage. It's harder to park near the apartments, especially because of the zone permits. So many parking tickets, so many of them contested."

Q "Don't even try. **There's always that one friend you have who drives,** so if you really need to make it somewhere, you could go ahead and ask a favor, but don't try parking. Even if you have a pass for one of the campus lots, they're often full."

Q "Parking on the street in Rogers Park is pretty easy if you do it before 7 or 8 p.m., watch for the permit signs though. And **there is a parking structure on the south side of the campus,** near Simpson, but if you live off campus, it's not always the most convenient option."

Q "There is **plenty of parking** for those who live in the dorms, and it's usually pretty easy to find a spot if you park off campus."

The College Prowler Take On...
Parking

Although some students inexplicably seem to have luck finding parking, it is advisable to take the advice of the great majority who do not. Parking in Chicago is a colossal undertaking worthy of an epic movie starring Al Pacino. If you find a spot, odds are that it will be nowhere near where you were trying to go. Sometimes it seems like it would be actually faster to walk places than to drive there and find parking. Campus lots fill up quickly. Street spots are scarce at best. Most students live close enough to campus that they do not need a car for their commute. Even if this was not so, Chicago's public transportation system can take you anywhere you want to go. If you need more reasons not to bring a car, think of today's poor emission standards and their effects on the environment.

With constant parking problems in mind along with the high price of gas within the city, and don't forget emission standards, it becomes clear that having a car on campus is more of an encumbrance than a luxury. Unless you absolutely need a car for some unfathomable reason, just leave it at home. Plus, everybody knows some fool who didn't take my advice and brought his '93 Taurus to school. Clunk around town in that instead, and save yourself a load of time, exasperation, and money.

The College Prowler™ Grade on
Parking: D-

A high grade in this section indicates that parking is both available and affordable, and that parking enforcement isn't overly severe.

Transportation

The Lowdown On...
Transportation

Ways to Get Around Town
On Campus

Loyola Shuttle Service, 7:30 a.m. – 11:00 p.m. (773) 508-6049

8-RIDE Escort Van, 5:30 p.m. – 1:00 a.m. (773) 508-RIDE

Public Transportation

Chicago Transit Authority (CTA)
(888) YOUR-CTA

Pick up train and bus schedules from the Loyola El Station. Loyola, like many Chicago universities, is part of the U-Pass program, which allows students to ride the El and any Chicago city bus as often as they like for one incredibly low fee, which is applied to their tuition each semester.

➡

Metra

(312) 322-6777

www.metrarail.com

The Metra train is the cheapest way to go between Chicago and the surrounding suburbs. Fares vary depending on the distance traveled. There are several stations in Chicago, but most trains originate from Union Station.

Taxi Cabs

American United Cab Association: (773) 248-7600

Blue Ribbon Taxi: (773) 878-5400

Checker Taxi: (312) CHECKER

Flash: (773) 561-4444

General Cab Co.: (773) 989-4800

Norshore Cab: (773) 743-0066

Car Rentals

Alamo, local: (773) 581-4531; national: (800) 327-9633, www.alamo.com

Avis, local: (312) 782-6827; national: (800) 831-2847, www.avis.com

Budget, local: (773) 686-6800; national: (800) 527-0700, www.budget.com

Dollar, local: (773) 735-7200; national: (800) 800-4000. www.dollar.com

Enterprise, local: (312) 494-3434; national: (800) 736-8222, www.enterprise.com

Hertz, local: (312) 951-2930; national: (800) 654-3131, www.hertz.com

National, local: (312) 236-2581; national: (800) 227-7368, www.nationalcar.com

Best Ways to Get Around Town:

Take the train. Loyola has an El stop within walking distance of campus, and the U-Pass program makes transit incredibly cheap for students.

Catch a bus. Chicago's buses go just about everywhere in the city, and while they're not as timely as the El, they too are covered by the U-Pass program.

Chicago is very **bike friendly**, with some streets having a bike lane running along the side. A beautiful lakefront path allows bikers to quickly move between the Lakeshore and Water Tower campuses.

Ways to Get Out of Town:

Airlines Serving Chicago:

Aer Lingus, (800) IRISH AIR, www.aerlingus.com

AeroMexico, (800) 237-6639, www.aeromexico.com

Air Canada, (888) 247-2262, www.aircanada.com

Air France, (800) 237-2747, www.airfrance.com

Alaska Airlines, (800) 252-7522

Alitalia, (312) 644-0404, www.alitalia.it

America West, (800) 235-9292, www.americawest.com

American Airlines, (800) 433-7300, www.americanairlines.com

Airlines (*Continued...*)

ATA, (800) I-FLY-ATA, www.ata.com

British Airways, (800) 247-9297, www.britishairways.com

British Midland, (800) 788-0555, www.flybmi.com

Continental, (800) 523-3273, www.continental.com

Delta, (800) 221-1212, www.delta-air.com

El Al, (312) 516-3525, www.elal.co.il

Iberia, (800) 772-4642, www.iberia.com

Japan Airlines, (800) 525-3663, www.japanair.com

Korean Air, (800) 438-5000, www.koreanair.com

LOT Polish Airlines, (312) 236-5501, www.lot.com

Lufthansa, (800) 645-3880, www.lufthansa.com

Northwest, (800) 225-2525, www.nwa.com

Spirit Airlines, (800)772-7117, www.spiritair.com

Southwest Airlines, (800) I-FLY-SWA

Swiss International Airlines, (877) 359-7947, www.swiss.com

Turkish Airlines, (800) 874-8875, www.flyturkish.com

United, (800) 241-6522, www.united.com

US Airways, (800) 428-4322, www.usairways.com

Airports:

O'Hare International Airport (ORD)

(800) 832-6352

www.ohare.com/o'hare

O'Hare International Airport is 15 miles and approximately 30 minutes by car from Loyola's Lakeshore Campus.

Midway International Airport

(773) 838-0600

www.ohare.com/midway

Midway Airport is 20 miles and approximately 32 minutes by car from Loyola's Lakeshore Campus.

How to Get There:

Chicago Transit Authority, (888) YOUR-CTA

The CTA Orange Line train runs directly to Midway, while the Blue Line will take you to O'Hare.

Continental Airport Express, (888) 284-3826

This airport shuttle will take you from downtown Chicago to O'Hare or Midway and back in about thirty minutes for $17.50.

A Cab Ride to the Airport Costs: $25

Greyhound

Chicago Greyhound Trailways
Bus Terminal
630 W. Harrison St.
Chicago, IL 60607
Local: (312) 408-5883
National: (800) 231-2222
www.greyhound.com
Chicago's Greyhound station
is located just west of the
Chicago River near Union
Station. It can easily be
reached from the Clinton stop
on the Blue Line El train.

Amtrak

Union Station
210 S. Canal St
Chicago, IL 60606
Local (Union Station): (312)
875-9696
National Amtrak: (800) USA-
RAIL
www.amtrak.com
Chicago's Amtrak trains run
out of historic Union Station
just west of the Chicago River,
blocks from the Quincy stop on
the Brown Line El train.

Travel Agents

STA Travel, 1160 North State
St., Gold Coast, (312) 951-0585

Travel With Us, 333 N.
Michigan Ave., Gold Coast,
(312) 372-1752

Apple Vacations, 1501 W.
Fullerton Ave., Lincoln Park,
(773) 880-0030

Students Speak Out On...
Transportation

{ **"Public transit is how you get around town. Included in your tuition is a pass for unlimited rides, something most of us will probably only truly appreciate after we graduate."**

Q "Loyola has its own stop on the El, take that DePaul and Northwestern. Getting from campus to downtown is a quick ride on the train. Loyola also offers **a shuttle between its main campus and its downtown campus** for students."

Q "The El is right next to campus, and with the U-Pass, t**he city is open to you** through public transportation."

Q "Thanks to numerous buses and the El, **you can get anywhere you want to go."**

Q "**Public Transportation is the only way to go**. I can't tell you enough how useful the U-Pass is. For a relatively small per-semester fee, you get unlimited rides on the El, Chicago's train system, and all city buses. In comparison, the cost of the pass for one semester wouldn't even buy you a month-long regular pass. The only drawback is that you're locked into purchasing it, whether you want it or not."

Q "The El will get you most anywhere, literally. **It may take just under an hour to make it to the South Side** to catch a White Sox game, but it won't cost you a dime. It would most likely take longer – and cost more, considering parking fees – were you to drive."

Q **"You don't need a car** in Chicago, and the hassle of finding parking only reinforces this. Then again, there are a lot of commuter students from the local Chicago area who don't live on campus, and a car may make more sense."

Q "It might take you a little while to get anywhere, but **you're pretty much dropped off at the door."**

Q "The Red Line El is your silver limousine, your ticket to the outer world, and your sociological experiment, all in one. **The best thing Loyola ever gave us is a U-Pass,** good for unlimited rides for each semester."

The College Prowler Take On...
Transportation

Chicago's public transportation system is one of the finest in the world. There is almost nowhere in the city that cannot be reached by train or bus. This is good news for Loyola students, for whom taking the train is almost cheaper than walking. For the amazingly low fee of $74 per semester, students get a CTA U-Pass, which gives them the ability to ride any CTA train or bus as often as they like. The handiness of this little plastic card cannot be underestimated: one ride on the CTA normally costs $1.75. Many students could easily spend more than $74 in a month riding the El back and forth between the university's two campuses. Many students assert that the U-Pass is the best part about going to Loyola.

Chicago is the hub of transportation throughout the Midwest. O'Hare International Airport has been voted the best in America six years running, and Midway is great for cheaper flights. Amtrak trains and Greyhound buses originating in Chicago travel all over the country. With so many different ways to get out of town, leaving the Windy City is so simple you could almost do it in your sleep.

The College Prowler™ Grade on
Transportation: A

A high grade for Transportation indicates that campus buses, public buses, cabs, and rental cars are readily-available and affordable. Other determining factors include proximity to an airport and the necessity of transportation.

Weather

The Lowdown On...
Weather

Average Temperature

Fall:	52 °F
Winter:	25 °F
Spring:	46 °F
Summer:	70 °F

Average Precipitation

Fall:	3.05 in.
Winter:	1.88 in.
Spring:	3.26 in.
Summer:	4.07 in.

Students Speak Out On...
Weather

{ **"The weather ranges from cold and windy in the winter, to warm and windy in the summer, to everything in between and windy the rest of the year."**

Q "You'll need to bring clothing for every season, and you'll need to keep the clothing for all the seasons. It's not odd for a summer day to peak at fifty-five one day, and hit ninety the next. Since Loyola is on Lake Michigan, **it's extremely windy** and it will be windy from every direction."

Q "Loyola is right on the lake so it gets windy. And it gets cold in the winter. And it snows, a lot. But **the spring, summer, and fall are great.** Jeans and a t-shirt for spring and fall, shorts and flip flops for the summer, and sweaters, hats, gloves, scarves, mittens, and long underwear for the winter. Don't forget to bring a Chicago Cubs t-shirt or hat. Real Loyola students are Cub fans."

Q "The first and last months of school will be great. The rest of the time it's winter with bitterly cold wind. **Full winter gear is required,** or prepare for a very long, very frostbitten six months."

Q "Midwest weather is always crazy, especially if you live in a city on a lake. Even if you plan on returning home to swap your winter clothes for your summer clothes before winter is scheduled to start, it's a very good idea to bring at least a few pieces of clothing for each season. **Chicago weather is as versatile as Madonna's wardrobe**, and changes just as frequently."

Q "The short answer is to pack literally everything in your wardrobe. If you're staying over the summer, it will most likely break 100 degrees at some point in July or August. In order to survive a windy Chicago winter with probable temps of zero and a wind chill of 20 degrees or so lower, layers and the full winter gear—hat, coat and scarf—are absolutely necessary. **Be prepared for anything**: there are often weeks where the temperature will change 30 or 40 degrees in the span of a few days."

Q "I love the Midwest because you get all four seasons, for better or worse. **The summer is really hot and muggy**. The winter is cruel, and they don't always plow the roads or sidewalks right away. And fall and spring are just right!"

Q **"Chicago weather is always fun.** You get weather as cold as Canada and weather as hot as Arizona."

Q "Chicago is blow-your-face-off freezing. For Loyola's sake they should change the school year to encompass summer and leave out winter entirely. **Don't bring an umbrella, it will blow inside out.** Instead, bring a raincoat. Don't bring beautiful leather shoes, they will become encrusted in ice and salt and goo. Instead, bring sneakers you don't give a rat's behind about."

Q **"Bring lots of layers,** something that goes over your ears, and stop caring about fashion for the months of December through March because by then everyone's too cold to care what the hell you look like. And if you weigh less than ninety pounds, fill your pockets with sand from the beach or you will blow away."

The College Prowler Take On...
Weather

Like most other aspects about Loyola, students maintain their sense of humor regarding the weather in the city they call home. Don't like the weather in Chicago? Wait five minutes, it will change. The negative is that the city is cold just about nine months out of the year. The positive is that with the constant wind dropping temperatures below zero on a regular basis, 50 degrees seems pretty temperate. You won't see many people with fancy hair dos in Chicago; the wind defies any amount of gel or mousse. Most people own a good collection of hats. You'll have to get used to wind burn rather than sun burn, because the wind blows directly into your face no matter which way you walk. Loyola's Lakeshore Campus is especially bad, because the entire area seems to have been built as one gigantic wind tunnel.

Students love and hate Chicago's fickle weather. During the winter, virtually no one ventures outside the dorms unless they have to. Summertime, however, brings the students outside in droves, looking to revel in the sunshine and their newfound ability to wear shorts. The best advice for someone new to Chicago is to simply accept the weather. It will change, unpredictably and frequently. So bring clothes for Siberia and for San Antonio; Chicago will feel like each at some point or another. Just make sure to go somewhere warm for Spring Break.

The College Prowler™ Grade on
Weather: D

A high Weather grade designates that temperatures are mild and rarely reach extremes, that the campus tends to be sunny rather than rainy, and that weather is fairly consistent rather than unpredictable.

Report Card Summary

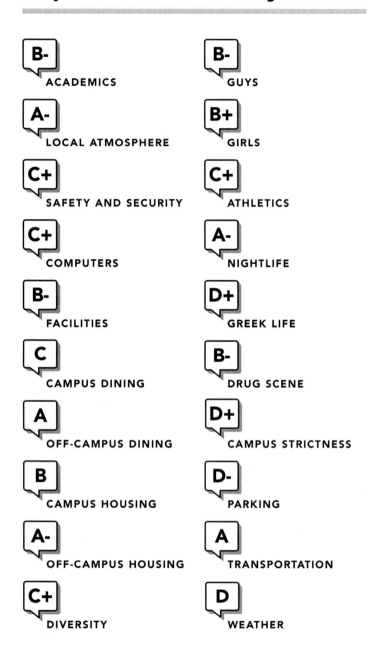

B-
ACADEMICS

A-
LOCAL ATMOSPHERE

C+
SAFETY AND SECURITY

C+
COMPUTERS

B-
FACILITIES

C
CAMPUS DINING

A
OFF-CAMPUS DINING

B
CAMPUS HOUSING

A-
OFF-CAMPUS HOUSING

C+
DIVERSITY

B-
GUYS

B+
GIRLS

C+
ATHLETICS

A-
NIGHTLIFE

D+
GREEK LIFE

B-
DRUG SCENE

D+
CAMPUS STRICTNESS

D-
PARKING

A
TRANSPORTATION

D
WEATHER

Overall Experience

Students Speak Out On...
Overall Experience

"Nothing beats the faculty, student body, and location, but the administration needs to get its act together. If they don't, there are plenty of other universities in Chicago to go to."

Q "The actual campus is awesome, the people are great, **the administration is Big Brother to the extreme**, and I wish I blew $50,000 playing one game of blackjack instead of going to Loyola."

"Hands down, the best part of Loyola is the people. **I met my best friends here**, and learned more from them about life then I did in any classroom. I wish I was at school elsewhere, but only because I finally know what I want to do with my life, and Loyola doesn't offer a program in that. Otherwise, I'm a Rambler and damn proud of it."

"I really enjoy Loyola. **The school is just the right size,** and having the city around is really great. Sometimes I do wish that I had gone somewhere with college football or a bigger party scene, but no matter where you go, there will always be something you are missing. Given everything that I gained by going to Loyola, I would never do it differently."

"Loyola still has **a lot of issues to sort out,** including the administration's seeming witch hunt for anything at all that could be wrong with student life, as well as some budget problems, but with ever-increasing class sizes, the financial problems should be a thing of the past."

"If you go to **Loyola's Rome campus** at any time during your college career, all the negative issues you may have had in Chicago just melt away like so much gelato."

"I think picked the right school for me, all things considered. Loyola, like any university, has its strengths and its weaknesses. **The Rome Center is awesome** and everyone should go. Also, it's worth saying that your college experience is what you make of it."

"While I know there are people who have bad experiences with Loyola, **I have had a great experience. You will get out of it what you put into it.**"

Q "I adore Loyola, because **all its faults just make you stronger and funnier,** and your friendships with other people who outlasted it become that much more solid. When it comes down to it, all colleges have the exact same problems. As long as the education is quality, which, brace yourself, it is at Loyola, who cares whether doing laundry is hard or the computer labs always have sticky keyboards. That's not what remains in your college memory. What you end up remembering about college is the friends you made, the professors who made you laugh and think, and the things you accomplished that you never would have imagined before you came."

The College Prowler Take On...
Overall Experience

Loyola's students are quick to point out the school's faults. There is little sugar-coating in their appraisal of the school as a financial mess that is so rife with incompetence that it is hard to accomplish even the simplest administrative tasks without putting up a fight. That said, most Loyolans love their school. They see its faults as nothing more than additional challenges they must face on their way to graduation. The majority of students would prefer to look past all the talk of budget cuts and program eliminations they hear during the course of their academic careers and focus on the positives. Loyola offers a quality education for those who are willing to work at it.

Are the administrative problems at Loyola disruptive to a student's studies? Definitely. Should this scare you away from Chicago's Jesuit institution? No. Loyola is starting to come slowly out of its period of financial distress. Fewer cutbacks are expected as incoming class sizes grow in size. Outside of the classroom, the university is actually growing and improving by the day. A new life sciences building is set to open in a couple of years, as is a state of the art dormitory. Most of the buildings around campus are slowly being renovated. The university has a feeling of newness to it, and this is a good thing for freshman just out of high school. Not only do you get a new beginning, but you get new facilities to make that start in. Many students who have graduated recently look at the campus improvements with jealousy, wishing they had been given the opportunity to make use of them. Students may be split on their feelings about Loyola, but it appears that the university is in the process of rebuilding itself anew. It is up to young scholars to follow suit.

The Inside Scoop

The Lowdown On...
The Inside Scoop

LUC Slang:

Know the slang, know the school. The following is a list of things you really need to know before coming to LUC. The more of these words you know, the better off you'll be.

LIE-ola: Local pronunciation for Loyola

SJ: Society of Jesus, the Catholic order which operates Loyola

LSC: Lakeshore Campus

WTC: Water Tower Campus

The RoPa, the Rog: Rogers Park, the neighborhood most Loyola students call home

The Ashtray: The area surrounding the statue of St. Ignatius Loyola behind Mertz Hall

CFSU: Centennial Forum Student Union, on the ground floor of Mertz Hall

SLLC: Simpson Living and Learning Center

Jez Rez: The lawn in front of Loyola's Jesuit Residence, where the priests live

➡

Sky: Skyscraper Building, the tallest at the LSC

Virgin Vault: Coffey Hall, Loyola's single sex female dorm

Hammies: Hamilton's Pub

The O: Oasis, a bar north of campus

Bruno's: Bruno and Tim's Lounge and Liquor Store

P Co.: The Pumping Company

Softball: Chicago sixteen-inch, definitely not fast-pitch

LSD: Not Lakeshore Drive, but Lakeshore Dining

Fr. Whatawaste: The name generally applied to any hot priest

RA: Resident Assistant

DR: Desk Receptionist

Granada Center: Former name for Fordham Hall

Lakefront: Former name for Santa Clara Hall

Kenmore: Former name for Rockhurst Halls North and South

The Red Line: The elevated train line that services Loyola

Things I Wish I Knew Before Coming to LUC

- Get on the smallest meal plan possible
- It's not a big party school
- Don't buy bed sheets from the school for their oversized beds
- How to manage my time better
- Take core classes first in case you change your mind about your major
- Try to avoid working full time while in school
- It's hard to get the administration to do anything without a fight
- If you want to study at the Rome Center, don't get written up

Tips to Succeed at LUC

• Pick classes you actually like

• Research professors before choosing your classes

• Actually go to class

• Do your homework yourself so you understand the material

• If you realize you don't like your chosen major, drop it sooner rather than later

• Always dispute bad grades

• Do all the readings, maybe you'll learn something from them

• Cultivate good study habits early on so you get into a working routine

• Don't stress out!

• Study at the Rome Center

LUC Urban Legends

• A frustrated priest murdered a nun on the top floor of Skyscraper Building. Her ghost supposedly still haunts the floor, to the delight of thrill-seeking students.

• Christina Aguilera almost went to college at Loyola.

School Spirit

School Spirit is almost nonexistent at Loyola. The lack of a football team really eliminates a huge possible rallying point for students. Still, when the basketball team plays well, students tend to get excited about the possibilities of an NCAA Tournament bid. Perhaps the most telling sign of the students' love for their school is their willingness to protest about it. Loyolans have such affection for their professors and academic programs that they are willing to fight the administration tooth and nail when it threatens them with cutbacks.

Traditions

The Loyola Ramblers vs. UIC Flames Basketball Game

The University of Illinois Chicago is Loyola's fiercest foe. In recent years, the rivalry was sparked by the play of two brothers: Loyola star David Bailey and his brother Martell.

The Sixth Man

A group of fanatical Rambler fans dressed in maroon and gold shirts attend every men's home basketball game. Whether the crowd is large or small, these guys spend more time trying to make people stand and cheer than the actual cheerleaders.

The Ides of March

Every year the Classics Club puts on its own little production of Julius Caesar's murder right around the middle of March. Performed in halting Latin, the performance is always entertaining, as students and teachers wearing bed sheets and grape leaves stumble through their lines and build comically to the ultimate slaying and occasional drenching in fake blood of their Caesar for the year.

Hunger Week

Sponsored by University Ministry, Hunger Week comes around once a year in October. Students work to heighten awareness in world hunger by fasting and doing service projects.

Late Night Breakfast

For one night, the Gentile Center becomes a gigantic greasy spoon, hosting students for a late night omelet and pancake extravaganza.

President's Ball

Once a year, Loyola puts on a celebration for its brightest and best to go and receive awards while wearing suits. P-Ball is the closest thing the university comes to having a homecoming dance, so if you like to get down to Rednexx and do the Macarena, strap on your dancing shoes and find yourself a ticket.

Finding a Job or Internship

The Lowdown On...
Finding a Job or Internship

Finding a job after graduation can be a daunting challenge in today's fluctuating economic climate. Loyola proposes to give its students and graduates a helping hand in their money making endeavors. The Career Center website, at www.luc.edu/resources/career, offers a job search service, the opportunity to post your resume so that prospective employers can search it, and links to other search sites. Offline, a whole staff of career advisors and employment counselors awaits your call at the Career Center office.

Advice

Many students overlook the Career Center's services while at the university. Don't make the same mistake. Even if you think you know everything there is to know about finding employment outside of the university, there is probably something you could stand to learn more about.

Career Center Resources & Services

- Campus employment
- Career Counseling
- Placement Advising
- Announcements of Job Fairs
- Graduate School Advising
- Resume and Cover Letter Writing Assistance
- Mock Interviews
- Job Search Website
- Training Seminars

Alumni

The Lowdown On...
Alumni

Website:
http://www.
loyolachicagoalumn.net

Office:
Alumni Office
Fifteenth Floor, Lewis Towers
820 N. Michigan Ave.
Chicago, IL 60611
luc-alum@luc.edu
(312) 915-7660
(800) 5-LOYOLA

Services Available

If you apply for an alumni card, you get access to Loyola's libraries, computer labs, and other facilities. You can pay to join Loyola's gym and to have the career center look for jobs for you. Plus, three times a year, you get a complimentary issue of Loyola Magazine.

Major Alumni Events

Although alumni are generally welcome to attend most events on campus, the most popular ones are basketball games and reunions. Before certain home games, alumni are invited to attend a reception with the players after the final whistle blows. Loyola also sponsors five and ten year reunions for its Chicago campuses, as well as more frequent get-togethers for students who studied in Rome.

Alumni Publications

Loyola Magazine comes out three times a year and is available both to students and alumni. The publication mostly does human interest stories about Loyola grads and current students, as well as alerting the community to events around campus.

Did You Know?

Famous LUC Alums

Bob Newhart, famous actor/comedian, star of a number of TV shows

William Daley, former U.S. Secretary of Commerce

Susan Candiotti, CNN correspondent

Richard A. Devine, former state's attorney for Cook County

Richard L. Flanagan, former CEO, Borders Books and Music

Neil F. Hartigan, former Illinois Attorney General

Don Novello, former writer and player on Saturday Night Live

Student Organizations

Some of Loyola's Student Organizations have websites, some do not. To find out more about an individual club, like contact information or history, check out Loyola's Student Life website at www.luc.edu/studentlife.

Alpha Epsilon Delta (AED) – Pre-med society Honor Society, www.luc.edu/orgs/aed

Alpha Kappa Psi – Business fraternity

Alpha Phi Omega – Service fraternity, www.geocities.com/apo_loyola/

American Chemical Society

American Medical Student Association - www.luc.edu/orgs/amsa

Amnesty International

Association for Computing Machinery - http://www.acm.luc.edu

Association of International Students in Education

Band of Wolves

Baseball Club – organizational email at loyola_baseball@luc.edu

Best Buddies

Beta Alpha Psi – Accounting fraternity

Beta Beta Beta – Biology fraternity, www.luc.edu/orgs/bbb

Beta Gamma Sigma – Honors fraternity

Beta Rho, Lambda Pi Eta – Communications fraternity

Big Brother Big Sister – organizational email at luc_bbbs@hotmail.com

Black Cultural Center (BCC)

Botanical Society

Business Dean's Advisory Council (BDAC) - www.sba.luc.edu/orgs/dac/

Cadence - www.geocities.com/cadenceluc

Campus Greens – organizational email at campus_greens@luc.edu

Campus Life at Water Tower (CLAW)

Campus Life Union Board (CLUB) - www.luc.edu/orgs/club

CAPTURE

Caribbean Student Union (CSU)

CFC Youth for Christ – organizational email at cfc_yfc_loyola@hotmail.com

Chardin Anthropological Society – organizational email at chardin_society@hotmail.com

Chi Alpha Christian Fellowship

Chinese American Student Association – organizational email at casa_love@hotmail.com

Chinese Students and

Scholars Association – organizational email at Loyola-CSSA@yahoogroups.com

Circle K - www.geocities.com/loyolacirclek

Citizens for Midwest Workers

Classics Club

College Bowl – organizational email at luccollegebowl@hotmail.com

College Democrats - www.geocities.com/lucdems/

College Republicans

Comparative Education Graduate Student Group - www.luc.edu/schools/education/ciegsa

Council of Pan-Asian Americans (COPAA) - www.luc.edu/orgs/copaa/

Criminal Justice Organization - www.luc.edu/orgs/crimjust/

Cycling Club - www.eteamz.com/luc-cycling/

Debate Society - www.luc.edu/orgs/debate

Delta Sigma Pi – Business fraternity, www.geocities.com/lucdfl

Diminuendo – organizational email at diminuendoluc@hotmail.com

Equestrian Association

Feminist Forum

French Club – organizational

email at frcluc@yahoo.com

Future Teachers of Chicago

Golden Key National Honor Society – organizational email at goldenkeyloyola@hotmail.com

Hellenic Student Association

Higher Education Student Association

Hillel - www.luc.edu/depts/ministry/hillel.html

Hindu Students Organization – organizational email at hsoloyola@hotmail.com

Honors Student Association

Human Resources Student Association - www.luc.edu/orgs/shrm/

Indian Students Association

International Association of Business Communicators - www.IABC.com

Irish American Student Association – organizational email at iasa@luc.edu

Italian Club

KAPWA Filipino Student Organization

Karate Club - www.shokidokarate.com/lukc

Korean Student Organization

Lacrosse Club - www.lax-cats.com/ramblax/index.php

Latin American Student Organization (LASO) - www.luc.edu/orgs/laso/

Loyola Lambdas

Loyola Phoenix Newspaper - www.luc.edu/phoenix

Loyola Students Against Sweatshops

Loyola University Bible Fellowship (LUBF)

Loyola University Chicago Tennis Club

Loyolacappella - www.luc.edu/orgs/loyolacappella

LU African American Student Association (LUASA)

LU Gospel Choir

Mathematics Club

Men's Rugby Club - www.luc.edu/depts/campusrec/mens_rugbyclub.html

Men's Volleyball Club - www.luc.edu/depts/campusrec/mens_vballclub.html

Mertz Hall Government

Middle Eastern Student Association - www.luc.edu/orgs/mesa/

Minority and Diversity Graduate Student Association

Minority Association of Pre-Health Students (MAPS) - www.luc.edu/orgs/maps/

Minority Men United - www.luc.edu/orgs/mmu

Minority Women United – organizational email at minoritywomenunited@hotmail.com

Model United Nations
- www1.luc.edu/depts/polisci/
ungrad/modelUN/un.html

Muslim Students Association
- www.luc.edu/orgs/msa

National Society of Collegiate
Scholars - www.nscs.org/

Neuroscience Club

Nursing Student Council

Orthodox Christian
Fellowship - www.luc.edu/
orgs/ocf

Philosophy Club

Physics Club – organizational
email at luc_physics_
club@yahoo.com

Pi Sigma Alpha – Honors
fraternity, www.luc.edu/depts/
polisci/ungrad/psa/psa.htm

Polish Students Alliance (PSA)
- www.luc.edu/orgs/polish/

Pre-Law Society
– organizational email at
prelawloyola@hotmail.com

Pre-Pharmacy Club

Pre-Veterinary Medicine Club

Pro-Life University Students
(PLUS) – organizational email
at plusloyola@hotmail.com

Psi Chi – National Psychology
honors society

Psychology Club

Rainbow Connection - www.
luc.edu/orgs/rainbow/

Rambler Apartment Assoc.

Real Estate Club

Residence Hall Government

- www.luc.edu/rhg

Simpson Hall Government

Sociology Club

South Asian Student Alliance
(SASA) - www.luc.edu/orgs/
sasa

Strategic Consulting Group

Student Athletic Advisory
Council

Student Dietetic Association
– organizational email at
loyolachicagosda@yahoo.
com

Student Environment Alliance

Student Nurses Association
of Illinois at Loyola (SNAI-L)

Students for a Sensible Drug
Policy

Tiawanese Student Assoc.

Unified Student Government
(USG) - www.luc.edu/orgs/usg

Vietnamese American
Student Association
– organizational email at
loyolalovesvasa@hotmail.com

Volunteer Action Program
(VAP) – organizational email
at vapluc@yahoo.com

Women's Rugby Club - www.
luc.edu/depts/campusrec/
womens_rugbyclub.html

Women's Soccer Club - www.
luc.edu/depts/campusrec/
soccerclub.html

vballclub.html

WLUW-FM, 88.7 Chicago
– Loyola's student-run radio
station, www.wluw.org

The Best & The Worst

The Ten BEST Things About LUC:

1	The Lakefront
2	Located in Chicago
3	The Rome Center and other study abroad programs
4	Guy/Girl ratio for guys
5	Beaches within walking distance
6	Simpson Dining Hall
7	Intramural sports
8	Student to teacher ratio
9	Good opportunities for service learning
10	Lots of student organizations

The Ten WORST Things About LUC:

1 Administrative red tape

2 Programs constantly downsized or eliminated

3 Guy/Girl ratio for girls

4 Lakeshore Dining Hall

5 No football team

6 Lack of positive fraternity presence

7 Rising cost of tuition

8 Nothing to do on campus

9 Constant Mertz Hall fire alarms

10 Poor athletic facilities

Visiting LUC

The Lowdown On...
Visiting LUC

HOTEL INFORMATION

Lincoln Park/Lakeview:
**Arlington House
International Hostel**
616 W. Arlington Pl.
Chicago, IL 60614
Phone: (773) 929-5380
Fax: (773) 665-5485
Toll Free: (800) HOS-TEL5
Distance from Campus: 7 miles
Price Range: $25 dorm, $55 private shared, $70 private single

The Belden-Stratford
2300 Lincoln Park West
Chicago, IL 60614
Phone: (773) 281-2900
Fax: (773) 880-2039
Toll Free: (800) 800-8301
Distance from Campus: 6.5 miles
Price Range: $109-$429

Best Western Hawthorne Terrace
3434 N. Broadway Ave.
Chicago, IL 60657
Phone: (773) 244-3434
Fax: (773) 244-3435
Toll Free: (888) 675-BEST
Website: www.
hawthorneterrace.com
Distance from Campus: 4.7 miles
Price Range: $100-$140

Days Inn Lincoln Park North
644 W. Diversey Pkwy.
Chicago, IL 60614
Phone: (773) 525-7010
Fax: (773) 525-6998
Toll Free: (888) LPN-DAYS
Email: info@lpndaysinn.com
Website: www.lpndaysinn.com
Distance from Campus: 5.7 miles
Price Range: $70-$80

Inn at Lincoln Park
601 W. Diversey Pkwy.
Chicago, IL 60614
Phone: (773) 348-2810
Fax: (773) 348-1912
Toll Free: (866) 774-7275
Website: www.innlp.com
Distance from Campus: 5.7 miles
Price Range: $79-$165

Gold Coast:

Allerton Crowne Plaza Hotel
701 N. Michigan Ave.
Chicago, IL 60611
Phone: (312) 440-1500
Fax: (312) 440-1819
Distance from Campus: 8.2 miles
Price Range: $75-$300

Best Western Inn of Chicago
162 E. Ohio St.
Chicago, IL 60611
Phone: (312) 787-3100
Fax: (312) 573-3140
Toll Free: (800) 557-2378
Website: www.innofchicago.com
Distance from Campus: 8.4 miles
Price Range: $77-$209

Cass Hotel
640 N. Wabash Ave.
Chicago, IL 60611
Phone: (312) 787-4030
Fax: (312) 787-8544
Toll Free: (800) 227-7850
Website: www.casshotel.com
Distance from Campus: 8.4 miles
Price Range: $79-$94

Chicago Marriott Downtown

540 N. Michigan Ave.
Chicago, IL 60611
Phone: (312) 836-0100
Fax: (312) 836-6929
Website: www.
chicagomarriottdowntown.
com
Distance from Campus: 8.4
miles
Price Range: $44-$145

Comfort Inn & Suites Downtown

15 E. Ohio St.
Chicago, IL 60611
Phone: (312) 894-0900
Fax: (312) 894-0999
Toll Free: (888) 775-4111
Website: www.
chicagocomfortinn.com
Distance from Campus: 8.6
miles
Price Range: $80-$270

Courtyard by Marriott Chicago Downtown

30 E. Hubbard St.
Chicago, IL 60611
Phone: (312) 329-2500
Fax: (312) 329-9452
Toll Free: (800) 321-2211
Distance from Campus: 9.3
miles
Price Range: $54-$275

Days Inn Gold Coast

1816 N. Clark St.
Chicago, IL 60614
Phone: (312) 664-3040
Fax: (312) 664-3048
Distance from Campus: 7.3
miles
Price Range: $59-$120

The Drake Hotel

140 E. Walton Pl.
Chicago, IL 60611
Phone: (312) 787-2200
Fax: (312) 787-1431
Website: www.thedrakehotel.
com
Distance from Campus: 8.5
miles
Price Range: $140-$805

Embassy Suites Hotel - Chicago Downtown

600 N. State St.
Chicago, IL 60610
Phone: (312) 943-3800
Fax: (312) 932-1000
Toll Free: (800) EMB-ASSY
Website: www.
embassysuiteschicago.com
Distance from Campus: 8.5
miles
Price Range: $109-419

Fairfield Inn and Suites Chicago Downtown

216 E. Ontario St.
Chicago, IL 60611
Phone: (312) 787-3777
Fax: (312) 787-8714
Distance from Campus: 8.9 miles
Price Range: $44-$145

Hampton Inn & Suites Chicago River North

33 W. Illinois St.
Chicago, IL 60610
Phone: (312) 832-0330
Fax: (312) 832-0333
Email: crn.sales@fhginc.com
Distance from Campus: 8.9 miles
Price Range: $170

Holiday Inn Chicago City Centre

300 E. Ohio St.
Chicago, IL 60611
Phone: (312) 787-6100
Fax: (312) 787-3055
Toll Free: (800) HOL-IDAY
Website: www.chicc.com
Distance from Campus: 8.5 miles
Price Range: $60-$125

Homewood Suites by Hilton Chicago-Downtown

40 E. Grand Ave.
Chicago, IL 60611
Phone: (312) 644-2222
Fax: (312) 644-7777
Distance from Campus: 9.2 miles
Price Range: $109-$249

Omni Chicago Hotel

676 N. Michigan Ave.
Chicago, IL 60611
Phone: (312) 944-6664
Fax: (312) 266-3015
Toll Free: (800) THE-OMNI
Distance from Campus: 8.2 miles
Price Range: $160-$270

Radisson Hotel & Suites Chicago

160 E. Huron St.
Chicago, IL 60611
Phone: (312) 787-2900
Fax: (312) 787-5158
Website: www.radisson.com/chicagoil
Distance from Campus: 8.3 miles
Price Range: $160-$340

Red Roof Inn
162 E. Ontario St.
Chicago, IL 60611
Phone: (312) 787-3580
Fax: (312) 787-1299
Toll Free: (800) 4MO-TEL6
Website: www.redroof.com
Distance from Campus: 9 miles
Price Range: $64-$80

Sheraton Chicago Hotel & Towers
301 E. North Water St.
Chicago, IL 60611
Phone: (312) 464-1000
Fax: (312) 464-9140
Website: www.
sheratonchicago.com
Distance from Campus: 9 miles
Price Range: $140-$3,500

Sofitel Chicago Water Tower
20 E. Chestnut St.
Chicago, IL 60611
Phone: (312) 324-4000
Fax: (312) 324-4026
Toll Free: (877) 813-7700
Url: http://www.sofitel.com
Distance from Campus: 8 miles
Price Range: $160-$460

The Westin Michigan Avenue Chicago
909 N. Michigan Ave.
Chicago, IL 60611
Phone: (312) 943-7200
Fax: (312) 943-9625
Website: www.
westinmichiganave.com
Distance from Campus: 7.8 miles
Price Range: $160-$2,500

Evanston

Hilton Garden Inn Evanston
1818 Maple Ave.
Evanston, IL 60201
Phone: (847) 475-6400
Fax: (847) 475-6460
Website: www.evanston.
gardeninn.com
Distance from Campus: 4.4 miles
Price Range: $130-$160

Margarita Inn
1566 Oak Avenue
Evanston, IL 60201
Phone: (847) 869-2273
Fax: (847) 869-2353
Distance from Campus: 4.2 miles
Price Range: $79-$150

Take a Campus Virtual Tour

www.ecampustours.com

Group Information Sessions or Interviews

The admissions staff generally schedules group informational sessions Monday through Friday at 10 a.m., 12:30 p.m., and 3 p.m. Saturday sessions begin at 12:15 p.m. All presentations last about an hour.

Campus Tours

Campus tours are available at both the Lakeshore and Water Tower campuses. Generally, tours are given Monday-Friday at 12:30 p.m., and Saturday at 12:15 p.m. To check times, call the Visit Coordinator before your visit. If you have a conflict with tour schedules, they may attempt to arrange one for you at a different time.

Overnight Visits

Overnight visits to Loyola are available to high school students at any of the university's residence halls while the school year is in progress. Prospective students stay over night with a student host and follow them around during their daily activities. An overnight visit is a great opportunity to get a feel for Loyola's lively community. Students are often willing to answer questions and offer advice to prospective Loyolans.

Scheduling

To schedule any of the above visits, call the Visit Coordinator on any week day between 8:30 a.m. and 5:00 p.m. CST at (773) 508-3075, or toll-free at (800) 262-2373. You can also complete the online visit form at www.luc.edu/undergrad/visitform.shtml, or email the admissions office at admission@luc.edu.

Directions to Campus

Driving from the North

- Take US-41 south to I-94.

- Follow I-94 east to Exit 39B, E. Touhy Ave.

- Merge onto E. Touhy Ave. Follow E. Touhy Ave. to N. Ridge Blvd. intersection

- Turn right onto N. Ridge Blvd. Follow N. Ridge Blvd. to W. Pratt Blvd. intersection.

- Turn left onto W. Pratt Blvd. Follow W. Pratt Blvd. to N. Sheridan Rd.

- Turn right onto N. Sheridan Rd. Follow N. Sheridan Rd. south to W. Loyola Avenue.

- Turn left onto W. Loyola Ave. and you'll be on campus.

Driving from the South

- Take I-55 Stevenson Expressway north to the US-41 N/Lakeshore Drive Exit on the left.

- Merge onto S. Lakeshore Drive. Follow Lakeshore Drive north until it becomes Hollywood Ave.

- Turn right onto N. Broadway St. Follow N. Broadway St. north until it becomes Sheridan Rd.

- Continue north on N. Sheridan Rd. to the W. Loyola Ave. intersection.

- Turn right onto W. Loyola Ave. and you'll be on campus.

Directions to Campus (*Continued...*)

Driving from the East

- Take I-90 west toward Chicago. Merge onto I-90 Express Lane W/I-94 Express Lane W/Dan Ryan Express Lane W via the exit on the left.

- Merge onto I-55 Stevenson Expressway via exit number 53C toward Lakeshore Drive.

- Take the US-41 N/Lakeshore Drive exit on the left.

- Merge onto Lakeshore Drive. Follow Lakeshore Drive until it becomes W. Hollywood Ave.

- Turn right onto N. Broadway St. Follow N. Broadway St. north until it becomes Sheridan Rd.

- Continue north on N. Sheridan Rd. to the W. Loyola Ave. intersection.

- Turn right onto W. Loyola Ave. and you'll be on campus.

Driving from the West

- Take I-90 east to Exit 84, Lawrence Ave./4800 N.
- Turn slight left onto W. Lawrence Ave.
- Turn left onto N. Cicero Ave./IL-50.
- Turn right on W. Foster Ave.
- Turn left onto US-14/N. Broadway St. Continue to follow N. Broadway St. until it becomes Sheridan Rd.
- Turn right onto W. Loyola Ave. and you'll be on campus.

Words to Know

Academic Probation – A student can receive this if they fail to keep up with their school's academic minimums. Those who are unable to improve their grades after receiving this warning can possibly face dismissal.

Beer Pong / Beirut – A drinking game with numerous cups of beer arranged in a particular pattern on each side of a table. The goal is to get a ping pong ball into one of the opponent's cups by throwing the ball or hitting it with a paddle. If the ball lands in a cup, the opponent is required to drink the beer.

Bid – An invitation from a fraternity or sorority to pledge their specific house.

Blue-Light Phone – Brightly-colored phone posts with a blue light bulb on top. These phones exist for security purposes and are located at various outside locations around most campuses. If a student has an emergency or is feeling endangered, they can pick up one of these phones (free of charge) to connect with campus police or an escort service.

Campus Police – Policemen who are specifically assigned to a given institution. Campus police are not regular city officers; they are employed by the university in a full-time capacity.

Club Sports – A level of sports that falls somewhere between varsity and intramural. If a student is unable to commit to a varsity team but has a lot of passion for athletics, a club sport could be a better, less intense option. If a club sport still requires too much commitment, intramurals often involve no traveling and a lot less time.

Cocaine – An illegal drug. Also known as "coke" or "blow," cocaine often resembles a white crystalline or powdery substance. It is highly addictive and dangerous.

Common Application – An application that students can use to apply to multiple schools.

Course Registration – The time when a student selects what courses they would like for the upcoming quarter or semester. Prior to registration, it is best to have an idea of several back-up courses in case a particular class becomes full. If a course is full, a student can place themselves on the waitlist, although this still does not guarantee entry.

Division Athletics – Athletics range from Division I to Division III. Division IA is the most competitive, while Division III is considered to be the least competitive.

Dorm – Short for dormitory, a dorm is an on-campus housing facility. Dorms can provide a range of options from suite-style rooms to more communal options that include shared bathrooms. Most first-year students live in dorms. Some upperclassmen who wish to stay on campus also choose this option.

Early Action – A way to apply to a school and get an early acceptance response without a binding commitment. This is a system that is becoming less and less available.

Early Decision – An option that students should use only if they are positive that a place is their dream school. If a student applies to a school using the early decision option and is admitted, they are required and bound to attend that university. Admission rates are usually higher with early decision students because the school knows that a student is making them their first choice.

Ecstasy – An illegal drug. Also known as "E" or "X," ecstasy looks like a pill and most resembles an aspirin. Considered a party drug, ecstasy is very dangerous and can be deadly.

Ethernet – An extremely fast internet connection that is usually available in most university-owned residence halls. To use an Ethernet connection properly, a student will need a network card and cable for their computer.

Fake ID – A counterfeit identification card that contains false information. Most commonly, students get fake IDs and change their birthdates so that they appear to be older than 21 (of legal drinking age). Even though it is illegal, many college students have fake IDs in hopes of purchasing alcohol or getting into bars.

Frosh – Slang for "freshmen."

Hazing – Initiation rituals that must be completed for membership into some fraternities or sororities. Numerous universities have outlawed hazing due to its degrading or dangerous requirements.

Sports (IMs) – A popular, and usually free, student activity where students create teams and compete against other groups for fun. These sports vary in competitiveness and can include a range of activities—everything from billiards to water polo. IM sports are a great way to meet people with similar interests.

Keg – Officially called a half barrel, a keg contains roughly 200 12-ounce servings of beer and is often found at college parties.

LSD – An illegal drug. Also known as acid, this hallucinogenic drug most commonly resembles a tab of paper.

Marijuana – An illegal drug. Also known as weed or pot; besides alcohol, marijuana is one of the most commonly-found drugs on campuses across the country.

Major –The focal point of a student's college studies; a specific topic that is studied for a degree. Examples of majors include physics, English, history, computer science, economics, business, and music. Many students decide on a specific major before arriving on campus, while others are simply "undecided" and figure it out later. Those who are extremely interested in two areas can also choose to double major.

Meal Block – The equivalent of one meal. Students on a "meal plan" usually receive a fixed number of meals per week.

Each meal, or "block," can be redeemed at the school's dining facilities in place of cash. More often than not, if a student fails to use their weekly allotment of meal blocks, they will be forfeited.

Minor – An additional focal point in a student's education. Often serving as a compliment or addition to a student's main area of focus, a minor has fewer requirements and prerequisites to fulfill than a major. Minors are not required for graduation from most schools; however some students who want to further explore many different interests choose to have both a major and a minor.

Mushrooms – An illegal drug. Also known as "shrooms," this drug looks like regular mushrooms but are extremely hallucinogenic.

Off-Campus Housing – Housing from a particular landlord or rental group that is not affiliated with the university. Depending on the college, off-campus housing can range from extremely popular to non-existent. Those students who choose to live off campus are typically given more freedom, but they also have to deal with things such as possible subletting scenarios, furniture, and bills. In addition to these factors, rental prices and distance often affect a student's decision to move off campus.

Office Hours – Time that teachers set aside for students who have questions about the coursework. Office hours are a good place for students to go over any problems and to show interest in the subject material.

Pledging – The time after a student has gone through rush, received a bid, and has chosen a particular fraternity or sorority they would like to join. Pledging usually lasts anywhere from one to two semesters. Once the pledging period is complete and a particular student has done everything that is required to become a member, they are considered a brother or sister. If a fraternity or a sorority would decide to "haze" a group of students, these initiation rituals would take place during the pledging period.

Private Institution – A school that does not use taxpayers dollars to help subsidize education costs. Private schools typically cost more than public schools and are usually smaller.

Prof – Slang for "professor."

Public Institution – A school that uses taxpayers dollars to help subsidize education costs. Public schools are often a good value for in-state residents and tend to be larger than most private colleges.

Quarter System (sometimes referred to as the Trimester System) – A type of academic calendar system. In this setup, students take classes for three academic periods. The first quarter usually starts in late September or early October and concludes right before Christmas. The second quarter usually starts around early to mid–January and finishes up around March or April. The last quarter, or "third quarter," usually starts in late March or early April and finishes up in late May or Mid-June. The fourth quarter is summer. The major difference between the quarter system and semester system is that students take more courses but with less coverage.

RA (Resident Assistant) – A student leader who is assigned to a particular floor in a dormitory in order to help to the other students who live there. A RA's duties include ensuring student safety and providing guidance or assistance wherever possible.

Recitation – An extension of a specific course; a "review" session of sorts. Because some classes are so large, recitations offer a setting with fewer students where students can ask questions and get help from professors or TAs in a more personalized environment. As a result, it is common for most large lecture classes to be supplemented with recitations.

Rolling Admissions – A form of admissions. Most commonly found at public institutions, schools with this type of policy continue to accept students throughout the year until their class sizes are met. For example, some schools begin accepting students as early as December and will continue to do so until April or May.

Room and Board – This is typically the combined cost of a university-owned room and a meal plan.

Room Draw/Housing Lottery – A common way to pick on-campus room assignments for the following year. If a student decides to remain in university-owned housing, they are assigned a unique number that, along with seniority, is used to choose their new rooms for the next year.

Rush – The period in which students can meet the brothers and sisters of a particular chapter and find out if a given fraternity or sorority is right for them. Rushing a fraternity or a sorority is not a requirement at any school. The goal of rush is to give students who are serious about pledging a feel for what to expect.

Semester System – The most common type of academic calendar system at college campuses. This setup typically includes two semesters in a given school year. The "fall" semester starts around the end of August or early September and finishes right before winter vacation. The "spring" semester usually starts in mid-January and ends around late April or May.

Student Center/Rec Center/Student Union – A common area on campus that often contains study areas, recreation facilities, and eateries. This building is often a good place to meet up with fellow students and is most commonly used as a hangout. Depending on the school, the student center can have a huge role or a non-existent role in campus life.

Student ID – A university-issued photo ID that serves as a student's key to many different functions within an institution. Some schools require students to show these cards in order to get into dorms, libraries, cafeterias, and other facilities. In addition to storing meal plan information, in some cases, a student ID can actually work as a debit card and allow students to purchase things from bookstores or local shops.

Suite – A type of dorm room. Unlike other places that have communal bathrooms that are shared by the entire floor, a suite has a private bathroom. Suite-style dorm rooms can house anywhere from two to ten students.

TA (Teacher's Assistant) – An undergraduate or grad student who helps in some manner with a specific course. In some cases, a TA will teach a class, assist a professor, grade assignments, or conduct office hours.

Undergraduate – A student who is in the process of studying for their Bachelor (college) degree.

ABOUT THE AUTHOR:

Nathan Ramin was in the process of putting the finishing touches on his Philosophy and Classical Studies degrees at Loyola when he learned about the opportunity to write for CollegeProwler. Although he was often uncertain what to think about his alma mater during his stay there, this book has given the author a much better perspective on things. In the end, he, like so many other students, loves Loyola, but was frustrated by the often maddening decisions made by the administration. Nate survived the school, however, and is actually surprised to admit that he is grateful to it for making him a stronger, more capable individual. He would like to continue working as a writer, and is currently looking for his next big project. Is grad school in the cards? Will Nate drop everything and move to Europe? Will the Tigers ever win the World Series again? Can our hero realize his lifelong dream to write for National Geographic Magazine? The author does not yet know the answer to these questions, but he can't wait to find out. Who knows, maybe you'll read about it all some day. He would of course be willing to answer any questions you might have for him about Loyola or the book, so feel free to email him at nathanramin@collegeprowler.com.

Thanks go out to Mom, Dad, Beezer, Nick, P.J., Katie, and to all of those awesome people who filled out questionnaires but whose names are, as promised, kept confidential. Finally, THANK YOU COLLEGEPROWLER!!!

Notes

....

....

....

....

....

....

....

....

....

....

....

....

....

Notes

....

....

....

....

....

....

....

....

....

....

....

....

....

Notes

....

....

....

....

....

....

....

....

....

....

....

....

....

....

Notes

....

....

....

....

....

....

....

....

....

....

....

....

....

....

Notes

....

....

....

....

....

....

....

....

....

....

....

....

....

Need More Help?

Do you have more questions about this school? Can't find a certain statistic? College Prowler is here to help. We are the best source of college information on the planet. We have a network of thousands of students who can get the latest information on any school to you ASAP. E-mail us at *info@collegeprowler.com* with your college-related questions. It's like having an older sibling show you the ropes!

Email Us Your College-Related Questions!

Check out **www.collegeprowler.com** for more details.
1.800.290.2682

Notes

....

....

....

....

....

....

....

....

....

....

....

....

....

Tell Us What Life Is Really Like At Your School!

Have you ever wanted to let people know what your school is really like? Now's your chance to help millions of high school students choose the right school.

Let your voice be heard and win cash and prizes!

Check out **www.collegeprowler.com** for more info!

Notes

....

....

....

....

....

....

....

....

....

....

....

....

....

....

Do You Have What It Takes To Get Admitted?

The College Prowler Road to College Counseling Program is here. An admissions officer will review your candidacy at the school of your choice and create a 12+ page personal admission plan. We rate your credentials with the same criteria used by school admissions committees. We assess your strengths and weaknesses and create a plan of action that makes a difference.

Check out **www.collegeprowler.com** or call 1.800.290.2682 for complete details.

COLLEGE PROWLER™

Notes

....

....

....

....

....

....

....

....

....

....

....

....

....

Pros and Cons

Still can't figure out if this is the right school for you?
You've already read through this in-depth guide; why not
list the pros and cons? It will really help with narrowing down
your decision and determining whether or not
this school is right for you.

Pros	Cons

Notes

....

....

....

....

....

....

....

....

....

....

....

....

....

Need Help Paying For School?

Apply for our Scholarship!

College Prowler awards thousands of dollars a year
to students who compose the best essays.
E-mail *scholarship@collegeprowler.com* for more
information, or call 1.800.290.2682.

Apply now at **www.collegeprowler.com**

Notes

....

....

....

....

....

....

....

....

....

....

....

....

....

Get Paid To Rep Your City!

Make money for college!

Earn cash by telling your friends about College Prowler!

Excellent Pay + Incentives + Bonuses

Compete with reps across the nation for cash bonuses

Gain marketing and communication skills

Build your resume and gain work experience for future career opportunities

Flexible work hours; make your own schedule

Opportunities for advancement

Contact *sales@collegeprowler.com*
Apply now at **www.collegeprowler.com**

Notes

....

....

....

....

....

....

....

....

....

....

....

....

....

Do You Own A Website?

Would you like to be an affiliate of one of the fastest-growing companies in the publishing industry? Our web affiliates generate a significant income based on customers whom they refer to our website. Start making some cash now! Contact *sales@collegeprowler.com* for more information or call 1.800.290.2682

Apply now at **www.collegeprowler.com**

Notes

....

....

....

....

....

....

....

....

....

....

....

....

....

Reach A Market Of Over 24 Million People.

Advertising with College Prowler will provide you with an environment in which your message will be read and respected. Place your message in a College Prowler guidebook, and let us start bringing long-lasting customers to you. We deliver high-quality ads in color or black-and-white throughout our guidebooks.

Contact Joey Rahimi
joey@collegeprowler.com
412.697.1391
1.800.290.2682

Check out **www.collegeprowler.com** for more info.

Notes

....

....

....

....

....

....

....

....

....

....

....

....

....

Write For Us!
Get Published! Voice Your Opinion.

Writing a College Prowler guidebook is both fun and rewarding; our open-ended format allows your own creativity free reign. Our writers have been featured in national newspapers and have seen their names in bookstores across the country. Now is your chance to break into the publishing industry with one of the country's fastest-growing publishers!

Apply now at **www.collegeprowler.com**

Contact *editor@collegeprowler.com* or
call 1.800.290.2682 for more details.

Notes

....

....

....

....

....

....

....

....

....

....

....

....

....